C1

Lincoln Township Library
2099 W. John Beers Rd.
Stevensville, MI 49127
429-9575

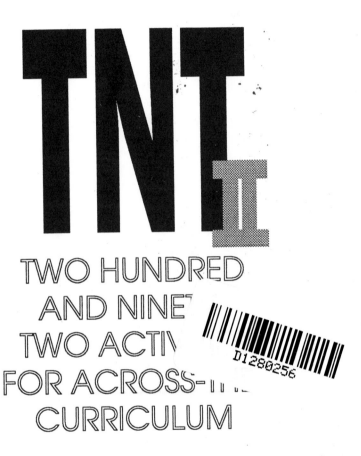

TNT II

TWO HUNDRED
AND NINET
TWO ACTIV
FOR ACROSS-THE
CURRICULUM

Eve Drury Geiger • Beverley Fonnesbeck

LINCOLN TOWNSHIP LIBRARY
2099 W. JOHN BEERS RD.
STEVENSVILLE, MI 49127
316-429-9575

Fearon Teacher Aids
Simon & Schuster Supplementary Education Group

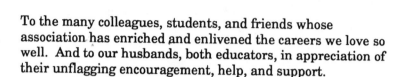

To the many colleagues, students, and friends whose association has enriched and enlivened the careers we love so well. And to our husbands, both educators, in appreciation of their unflagging encouragement, help, and support.

Editor: Susan J. Kling
Copyeditor: Lisa Schwimmer
Illustration: Tracy La Rue Hall
Design: Diann Abbott

Entire contents copyright © 1991 by Fearon Teacher Aids, part of the Education Group of Simon & Schuster, a Paramount Communications company. However, the individual purchaser may reproduce designated materials in this book for classroom and individual use, but the purchase of this book does not entitle reproduction of any part for an entire school, district, or system. Such use is strictly prohibited.

ISBN 0-86653-995-6

Printed in the United States of America

1.9 8 7 6 5 4 3 2 1

CONTENTS

INTRODUCTION

Activities in this book have been designed to emphasize the correlation between language arts, social studies, science, and other curriculum areas. We believe that education is a learning process by which children learn to function and make sense of the world. Students need to recognize relationships among their class subjects to accomplish this goal.

This book is divided into several sections. The first section contains general activities that can be used in many class lessons to enhance the learning process. After the title of each activity is the specific skill or skills the activity emphasizes.

The second section is devoted to themes. Suggestions are given to help the teacher set up and run theme units effectively. Book lists are included at the end of each theme section.

Emphasis has been placed throughout this book on student research and reference work. The ability to access and process information is essential in today's world. Activities encourage the use of reference materials, dictionaries, encyclopedias, and libraries.

The examples and suggested readings are intended to assist teachers in adapting the ideas to the students, subject matter, and materials available. Many of the recommended books are available in school and public libraries. Consultation with librarians will add many books to the lists.

Many of the activities in our collection are original. Many more have been gathered over the years from colleagues at the elementary and secondary teaching levels and from students enrolled in our university classes. We acknowledge a particular debt to the Bay Area and Anchorage Writing Projects.

GENERAL ACTIVITIES

After the name of each activity is a description of what the activity is all about—creative writing, reading, dramatic expression, research, and so on. When appropriate, recommended readings follow each activity listing as well.

1

Add a Chapter (reading, creative writing)
Read a historical novel to the class or have students read their own historical novels. Have students write an additional chapter that involves the main character in a new episode.

Recommended Books

Beatty, Patricia. *Be Ever Hopeful, Hannalee.* New York: Morrow, 1988.

Beatty, Patricia. *Turn Homeward, Hannalee.* New York: Morrow, 1984.

Bulla, Clyde Robert. *The Sword in the Tree.* New York: Crowell, 1956.

Clapp, Patricia C. *Constance.* New York: Penguin, 1986.

Harvey, Brett. *Cassie's Journey: Going West in the 1860s.* New York: Holiday, 1987.

Hautzig, Esther. *The Endless Steppe.* New York: Harper & Row, 1987.

Konigsburg, E. L. *A Proud Taste for Scarlet and Minier.* New York: Dell, 1985.

Siegel, Scott. *Revenge of the Falcon Knight*. New York: Avon, 1985.

Speare, Elizabeth George. *The Sign of the Beaver*. Boston: Houghton Mifflin, 1983.

2

Adopt a Whale (research, creative writing)
To create interest in sea life, suggest that students write to International Wildlife Coalition, The Whale Adoption Program, 634 North Falmouth Highway, Box 388, North Falmouth, MA 02556, for information on adopting a whale.

3

Advertisements (reading, creative writing, art)
Have students compose advertisements for historical novels. Encourage the use of descriptive words and graphic illustrations to encourage the reading of the books.

Recommended Books

Collier, James and Collier, Christopher. *My Brother Sam Is Dead*. New York: Macmillan, 1974.

Fox, Paula. *The Slave Dancer*. New York: Bradbury, 1973.

Graeber, Charlotte T. *Grey Cloud*. New York: Macmillan, 1979.

MacLachlan, Patricia. *Sarah, Plain and Tall*. New York: Harper & Row, 1985.

O'Dell, Scott. *The King's Fifth*. Boston: Houghton Mifflin, 1966.

4

Advertising Posters
(research, reference, speaking, art)
Have students design posters to sell an idea or a product. Encourage the use of large, colorful pictures and designs with simple texts. Posterboard with colored cutouts or tempera paint might also be used. Ask the artists to explain their advertising strategies. Or suggest that the class try to determine the strategy before hearing the explanation. Some strategies include posters to:

- attract sailors to an explorer's ship
- attract immigrants to a certain place
- encourage people to buy a product of the past
- advertise a festival
- broadcast a change in a law
- announce an event, such as a chariot race or a marathon

5

Advertising Propaganda (listening, creative writing)
Have students watch an evening television program and take notes on the advertisers' slogans for the commercials. Ask the students to share their notes with the class, but not to say what the product is. See if anyone can identify the product being sold. Discuss the propaganda strategies that are used. Encourage students to write slogans advertising an imaginary product. Share the slogans with the class to determine if they can identify the strategies used.

6

Agricultural Progress (reference, research)
As a class project, analyze and document why progress in agriculture has been uneven throughout the world. Relate the progress to the environment (geographic features, climate, natural resources, and people). Make a class chart and record the information gathered. Save one large column for the results (goods, crops, produce, exports). This project may run for a period of time so that information may be added to the chart. Suggest that a group of students research how scientific discoveries have improved agricultural conditions in some regions.

Recommended Books

Patterson, Geoffrey. *Dairy Farming.* Bergenfield, NJ: Andre Deutsch, 1984.

Rahn, Joan. *More Plants That Changed History.* New York: Macmillan, 1982.

7

Alphabet Action (creative thinking, creative writing, art)
The following activities are for children of all ages. Older children may work alone, while younger children may need some help. Give each student one letter of the alphabet to work with. Encourage the students to:

- make their letters into an animal figure.
- browse through alphabet storybooks. Then design a page using just their letters.
- draw a picture of an object whose name starts with their letters.
- write a noun that begins with their letters. Illustrate the noun.
- write a limerick or nursery rhyme about a historic person whose name begins with their letters. Illustrate the limerick or nursery rhyme.

When all the letters have been illustrated, bind the pages in a book for the classroom library.

Recommended Book

Anno, Mitsumasa. *Anno's Alphabet: An Adventure in Imagination.* New York: Crowell, 1975.

8

Analyze a Newspaper Article (interpretative reading)
Find an article on the same story in several local newspapers. Make copies of the articles for the students. Have students analyze and compare the way each newspaper handles the story. Help students find biases, inferences, innuendos, and other shades of meaning. Compare the use of techniques by the different news writers.

9

Ancestor Map (research, illustrative reporting)
On the borders of a large world map, place a snapshot of each student. Have students research their families' origins. Ask students to write a short biography of themselves to place beside their photographs. Attach strings from the photos to the countries of their origin. Encourage students to research the native dress of the country as well. Suggest that students make small figures in native dress. These figures may be cutouts or drawings.

10

Animal Poems (creative poetry)
With the class, write a poem about a famous animal. Then have students choose a famous animal of their

own to create a poem about. The poem might be written as if the animal were actually speaking. Use imaginary animals if real ones are unknown. Examples:

• Paul Revere's horse
• Alexander the Great's horse
• Martha Washington's cat
• Cleopatra's bird

An Antique Collection (research)

11

Collect several antique items that are not used today—for example, large ice tongs, wooden cheese boxes, butter molds, and cylinder records. Encourage students to bring objects from home, borrow from friends, or search the flea markets and garage sales. Have students draw pictures and write brief descriptions of the items collected. Arrange the drawings and descriptions on a bulletin board.

Architectural Relationships (reading, research, composition)

12

Gather pictures of public buildings around the world from different time periods. Have students choose one building to research. Ask students to prepare a paper that discusses the relationship between the society represented and the style and materials used in the construction of the building. This may be done in groups or as individual projects. Have students share papers with the class to see if all agree with the conclusions that have been drawn. A follow-up experience might be to study the influence of the past on architecture today.

Recommended Books

Isaacson, Phillip M. *Round Buildings, Square Buildings, and Buildings That Wiggle Like a Fish.* New York: Knopf, 1988.

Kimmel, Eric. *Nicanor's Gate.* Philadelphia: Jewish Publication Society, 1979.

Macaulay, David. *City: A Story of Roman Planning and Construction.* Boston: Houghton Mifflin, 1983.

13

Art or Architectural Comparison (reference, research, comparison, art)
As a class, construct a chart comparing two types of art or architecture. Ask students to illustrate the differences with drawings, paintings, or cutouts, and write explanations for the type displayed. Examples:

- Egyptian versus Mayan art
- Greek versus Roman art
- Chinese versus Japanese architecture
- Eskimo versus Native American architecture

Recommended Books

Cesarani, Gian Paolo. *Grand Constructions.* New York: Putnam, 1983.

Giblin, James Cross. *Skyscraper Book.* New York: Crowell, 1981.

Isaacson, Phillip. *Round Buildings, Square Buildings, and Buildings That Wiggle Like a Fish.* New York: Knopf, 1988.

Macaulay, David. *Cathedral: The Story of Its Construction.* Boston: Houghton Mifflin, 1973.

14

Arts and Crafts Exhibit (research, illustrative reporting)
With the class, organize an exhibit of arts and crafts from a selected country or culture. Use prints or replicas of masterpieces. Help students place the articles and prints in an attractive display. Ask students to write brief descriptions of the artists and the works. Select guides to conduct tours of the exhibit for other classes and visitors. Visit an art museum, if possible.

Recommended Book

St. Tamara. *Asian Crafts.* San Diego, CA: Lion, 1972.

15

Automation Investigations (research, illustrative reporting, outlining)
A group of students may find it interesting to investigate the advantages and disadvantages of automation.

The use of periodical literature would be helpful for this type of research. Have participants give demonstrations to present their findings. A brief written outline of main points may be helpful for the audience.

16

Barter and Trade (research, dramatic expression)
Divide the class into groups of two or three students. Have the groups present a dramatization showing the difficulties of trading by means of barter and the convenience of trading with money. Encourage students to devise skits with two scenes presenting "Yesterday" and "Today." The first scene should show bartering in the past and the second a scene of trade in the modern world. As an extension of this activity, a group may wish to research the beginnings of coinage and the development of monetary systems. Another group may wish to demonstrate how trade might be handled in the future.

17

Book Awards (literature, evaluation, letter writing)
Have your class nominate and choose a book for a historical fiction award similar to the Newbery or Caldecott. Help students list book requirements for these two awards, as well as the requirements for their own historical fiction award. Allow a week or so for nominations by the class. Have a nominations ceremony in which children explain their reasons for nominating a particular book. When nominations are complete, share the books with the class by reading each book aloud over a period of several weeks. Have children prepare voting ballots and vote for the book of their choice. The first, second, and third place winners might be tallied. Ask groups of students to make ribbons for the winners, book posters for the library, write an article for the school newspaper, and write letters to the winning authors and illustrators.

18

Book Character Visit (reading, letter writing)
Invite a favorite historical book character to visit the classroom for a week. With the class, develop activities based on the life of the character. Help students create a bulletin-board display about the historical character. Include drawings of the character's clothing, personal effects, and surroundings. Have students write letters to friends describing the week's activities and the visitor's

reaction to modern times. Encourage the children to share their letters with each other for discussion and comparison.

Recommended Books

De Angeli, Marguerite. *The Door in the Wall*. New York: Scholastic, 1984.

Gates, Doris. *Blue Willow*. New York: Penguin, 1976.

Gray, Elizabeth. *Adam of the Road*. New York: Penguin, 1987.

Hamilton, Virginia. *The House of Dies Drear*. New York: Macmillan, 1968.

Hunt, Irene. *Across Five Aprils*. New York: Berkley, 1987.

MacLachlan, Patricia. *Sarah, Plain and Tall*. New York: Harper & Row, 1985.

Snyder, Zilpha Keatley. *And the Condors Danced*. New York: Berkley, 1986.

19

Book Characters' Viewpoints (interpretative reading, dramatic expression)

Ask a few students to choose book characters that lived at about the same time and share the book characters' feelings and viewpoints. Encourage the participants to dress like the characters selected. The costumes will help the rest of the class recognize the characters.

Recommended Books

Bergman, Tamar. *The Boy from Over There*. Boston: Houghton Mifflin, 1988.

Forbes, Esther. *Johnny Tremain*. New York: Dell, 1969.

Fritz, Jean. *Brady*. New York: Putnam, 1960.

Greene, Bette. *Summer of My German Soldier*. New York: Bantam, 1984.

Reit, Seymour. *Behind Rebel Lines: The Incredible Story of Emma Edmunds, Civil War Spy*. San Diego: Harcourt Brace Jovanovich, 1988.

Richter, Hans P. *Friedrich*. New York: Penguin, 1987.

Uchida, Yoshiko. *Journey to Topaz*. Fort Lauderdale: Creative Arts, 1985.

Yolen, Jane. *The Devil's Arithmetic*. New York: Viking, 1988.

20

Book Friends Around the World (literature, oral expression, art)

Collect and display books about other countries. Have each child select a book to read. On butcher paper, have the children trace around each other to make life-size drawings of the main characters of their books. Have the paper characters sit around a table to tell their stories and ask each other questions. The children should be seated behind the paper characters to answer questions about the setting and events of their stories. Develop a TV program or short skit with theme music from the countries represented. Background scenes might be drawn and hung behind the characters. If a video camera is available, you might wish to make a film.

Book Jacket (reading, illustrative reporting) Ask students to design book jackets for their favorite historical novels. Provide the class with paper folded to look like a book jacket. Encourage the students to write a short synopsis of the story on the front inside flap and a brief biography of the author on the back cover. Ask the students to illustrate the jacket front to interest other readers. Arrange the book jackets on a bulletin board in the classroom or library. Or put the book jackets on the novels and display the books in the classroom library.

21

Recommended Books

Banks, Lynne Reid. *Indian in the Cupboard.* New York: Doubleday, 1985.

Banks, Lynne Reid. *Return of the Indian.* New York: Doubleday, 1986.

Blos, Joan. *A Gathering of Days: A New England Girl's Journal, 1830-32.* New York: Macmillan, 1979.

Freedman, Russell. *Buffalo Hunt.* New York: Holiday, 1988.

Lunn, Janet. *The Root Cellar.* New York: Scribners, 1983.

McDonald, Joyce. *Mail-Order Kid.* New York: Putnam, 1988.

O'Dell, Scott. *Island of the Blue Dolphins.* Boston: Houghton Mifflin, 1960.

Snyder, Zilpha K. *The Egypt Game.* New York: Atheneum, 1967.
Yep, Laurence. *Mountain Light.* New York: Harper & Row, 1985.

Borrowed Language (vocabulary)

Help the class collect common words and phrases that come from other countries. Construct a chart showing the words or phrases, origins, and their meanings.

22   Examples:

• scone	Scotland	round, soft, doughy pastry
• déjà vu	France	already seen
• stoop	Holland	small porch
• bon voyage	France	good trip
• napoleons	France	cream-filled, iced pastries

Recommended Books

American Heritage Dictionary Editors. *American Heritage Dictionary.* Boston: Houghton Mifflin, 1985.
American Heritage Dictionary Editors. *Word Mysteries and Histories: From Quiche to Humble Pie.* Boston: Houghton Mifflin, 1987.

Build a Model (research, illustrative reporting, art)

Have students build models or draw diagrams of historic inventions. Suggest that students prepare a written explanation that describes the construction and its functions. Help the students organize a Science Fair to display the finished products. Set a special time for visitor viewing and lectures by the participants.

23

Examples:

- Fulton's steamboat
- covered wagon
- cotton gin
- telephone
- crossbow

- log cabin
- early phonograph
- first printing press
- first horseless carriage
- Wright brothers' plane

Recommended Books

Aaseng, Nathan. *The Inventors: Nobel Prizes in Chemistry, Physics, and Medicine.* Minneapolis: Lerner, 1988.

Crump, Donald J. *Small Inventions That Make a Big Difference.* Washington, D.C.: National Geographic, 1984.

24

A Business Letter (research, letter writing)
While studying careers of a specific region, have students pretend to work at a particular job. Discuss the aspects of various jobs. Then ask students to write letters to a worker with the same job in another country. Suggest that the writers describe their work situations and the difficulties and advantages of the job. Encourage students to share their letters with others.
Examples:
- sheepherder in the United States to a sheepherder in Australia
- fisherman in Norway to a fisherman in Alaska
- citrus grower in Florida to a citrus grower in Spain
- cheesemaker in Switzerland to a cheesemaker in Wisconsin
- Mexican rugmaker to a Native American rugmaker

25

Catchy Headlines (main idea)
Collect news items that have eye-catching headlines. Cut the headlines off the news articles, mark the backs or make an answer key, and place the headlines and articles in separate envelopes. Distribute two or three news items to each student. Ask the students to write a new headline for each article. Compare the headlines with the originals to see if both emphasize the main idea.

26

Causes and Results (interpretative reading)
As a review for a country or historic period, create a chart of the causes and results of conflict. Help the students look at the founding and progressive development of the country, time period, and the reasons for successes and failures. This may be done with small groups, followed by a sharing period to coordinate efforts and fill in the chart.

27

Celebrations (creative writing)
Share a book about celebrations with the class. After reading the book, try these ideas:

- Ask children to share a special experience in nature that they remember. Help the children name the days, such as "Snake in the Garden Day" or "Soaked in the Rain Day."
- During one week, help children list special happenings related to nature that they would like to celebrate. At the end of the week, ask the children to choose their favorite nature experience and write a poem about it.
- Take children on a nature walk. Celebrate finding pawprints in the snow, hearing or seeing a particular bird, and noticing signs of the season.

Recommended Books

Bauer, Caroline F. *Celebrations: Read-Aloud Holiday and Theme Book Programs.* New York: Wilson, 1985.

Baylor, Byrd: *I'm in Charge of Celebrations.* New York: Scribners, 1986.

28

Cereals (research, report writing, generalizations)
Ask students to bring empty cereal boxes to school. Record the various grains on a chart labeled "cereals." Ask one group of students to research where the grains are grown and record the findings on the chart. Encourage several students to write to the consumer addresses found on the cereal packages, asking where the cereal is processed. The results can be recorded on the chart. Ask for volunteers to research the nutritional value of each cereal to determine which is the most wholesome. Encourage the groups to summarize their work and present their findings to the class.

Recommended Books

Aliki. *Corn Is Maize: The Gift of the Indians.* New York: Harper & Row, 1976.

McDermott, Gerald. *Daughter of Earth: A Roman Myth.* New York: Delacorte, 1984.

29

A Character's Diary (creative writing)
Ask students to assume the roles of favorite book characters. Choose one character and discuss the type of diary entries that character might write. Ask the students to keep a diary for ten days as if they were their character. Remind students to keep in mind what is known about the story setting, the character's general nature, and reactions to various situations.

Recommended Books

Blos, Joan. *A Gathering of Days: A New England Girl's Journal, 1830-32.* New York: Macmillan, 1979.

Brenner, Barbara. *Wagon Wheels.* New York: Harper & Row, 1978.

Dillon, Eilis. *The Seekers.* New York: Macmillan, 1986.

Harvey, Brett. *My Prairie Years: Based on the Diary of Elenore Plaisted.* New York: Holiday, 1986.

Holling, Holling C. *Tree in the Trail.* Boston: Houghton Mifflin, 1942.

Lewis, Elizabeth F. *Young Fu of the Upper Yangtze.* New York: Holt, 1973.

Lowry, Lois. *Number the Stars.* Boston: Houghton Mifflin, 1989.

Speare, Elizabeth George. *The Sign of the Beaver.* Boston: Houghton Mifflin, 1983.

Wilder, Laura Ingalls. *Little House in the Big Woods.* New York: Harper & Row, 1953.

A Character's Travels (reading, illustrative reporting)

30 Have students trace the travels of characters in historical novels on large sheets of drawing paper. Suggest that students draw small pictures to show the various stops made by the characters. Ask students to label the pictures and write the names of the books and authors on the map. Display the maps along a school hallway.

Recommended Books

Fleischman, Sid. *The Whipping Boy.* New York: Greenwillow Books, 1986.

Kroeber, Theodora. *Ishi, Last of His Tribe.* New York: Bantam, 1973.

Lunn, Janet. *The Root Cellar.* New York: Scribners, 1983.

Moeri, Louise. *Save Queen of Sheba.* New York: E. P. Dutton, 1990.

Treece, Henry. *Viking's Dawn.* Chatham, NY: S. G. Phillips, 1956.

Vander Els, Betty. *The Bomber's Moon*. New York: Farrar, Straus and Giroux, 1984.

Wisler, G. Clifton. *This New Land*. New York: Walker, 1987.

Yates, Elizabeth. *Carolina's Courage*. Greenville, SC: Bob Jones University, 1989.

City Research (research, report writing)

31

Have students choose a city to research. Discuss what types of information to look for. Information that might be included: location, origin, growth, development, outstanding features, and current problems of the city. Suggest that students use newspapers, magazines, and travel guides as sources of information. Have students write city reports based on their research. Encourage students to share their reports with others in the classroom.

A Class Acrostic (vocabulary)

Create a class acrostic using only historical terms related to a recent area of study. Start with a long historical term. For each letter, write a related word. For example:

32

Manor house
Icon
Duke
Drawbridge
Lance
England

Armor
Guild
Empire
Serf

33 **A Class Book of Fruits and Vegetables** (research, reporting)

Compiling a class book of fruits and vegetables of a

state, country, or region offers an opportunity for practicing simple research and reporting skills. Suggest that small groups of students research the fruits and vegetables grown in a specific area. Encourage the students to be creative in how they report their findings to the class. Pictures may be drawn and colored or cut from magazines for illustration. As an additional activity, have students research how the products are grown and taken to market.

Recommended Books

Johnson, Sylvia A. *Apple Trees*. Minneapolis: Lerner, 1983.
Turner, Dorothy. *Potatoes*. Minneapolis: Carolrhoda, 1989.

34

Class Mobile (research, visual summary)
As a class, construct a mobile that shows the countries of origin represented by the students in the classroom. Have children draw outlines of the countries. Suspend the countries from coat hangers or wire frames. As a variation, the students might show crops grown in a country, exports, or types of transportation on the outlines. Pictures representing historical stories could also be placed on the mobiles.

35

Class Time Capsule (creative thinking)
Begin this activity in the first week of school and open the capsule during the last week of school. Discuss with the class the purpose of a time capsule. Brainstorm what to put in a class time capsule. Some ideas might include:

- diary entries for the first week of school
- tape recordings of the class reading stories
- photographs of the class
- writing samples of the class

As a class, select a capsule—a large plastic jar, a shoebox, or a cigar box, for example. Plan a ceremony and seal the capsule. Throughout the school year, refer to the time capsule when appropriate.

Cloth Design (research, composition)
On a sheet of paper, have children draw and color designs for cloth woven in a particular country or region that they have researched. Encourage students to write descriptions of the design and its importance. Also ask children to explain the type of fabric and the weaving process. Examples:

36

- tapa cloth from Hawaii
- plaids from Scotland
- silks from China
- madras from India

Recommended Books

Lasky, Kathryn. *The Weaver's Gift*. New York: Warne, 1984.
Miles, Miska. *Annie and the Old One*. Boston: Little, Brown, 1972.

Coat of Arms (research, illustrative reporting, art)
Have students design coat of arms, shields, brands, or logos for a family or business. Provide the class with crayons, watercolors, markers, and colored paper for their designs. Then have students write descriptions of the design and its meaning. Examples:

37

- crusader's shield
- ranch brand
- early cloth manufacturer
- English or French nobleman
- Spanish don

Recommended Books

Byam, Michele. *Arms and Armor*. New York: Knopf, 1988.
Gibson, Michael. *Knights*. New York: Arco, 1979.
Scarry, Huck. *Looking into the Middle Ages*. New York: Harper & Row, 1985.
Wilkinson, Frederick. *Arms and Armor*. New York: Watts, 1984.

Comic Books Versus Original Novels (evaluation, drawing conclusions)

38

Some classics have been written in comic book form or as shortened versions of the original. Collect as many examples as possible. Have students compare the comic books and shortened versions to the original novels. Then ask students to list the differences.

A Communications Exposition (research, oral expression)
Organize a Communications Exposition. Arrange the class in small groups to research selected topics, such as radio, television, computers, telephones, and newspapers. Assign each group an area of the room or bulletin-board space to display illustrations related to their topic. Have each group prepare oral presentations of the information gathered. This may be a demonstration, a skit, an illustrated talk, or any other creative activity. Invite guest speakers from the media, telephone company, or computer firms to participate in the exposition.

39

A Contest (research, reporting)
As a review at the end of a study, have the class imagine a great contest is to be held and that they are the contestants. The participants must visit every state or province in the country and purchase a product from that place. The contestants must take the product to the next state or province and trade for a new product. This activity continues until every state or province has been visited. Have the students trace the route on a map, and as each place is visited, record the product on the map. The contestants might keep a log of each day's travel and record the exchanges made. Additional tasks may be added by increasing the number of goods exchanged.

40

Contrast Then and Now (literature, comparing and contrasting)
After the children have read a historical story, provide sheets of paper divided into two columns. Ask the

41

children to compare the way tasks or jobs were done in the past with the way these activities are done today. A few tasks include washing clothing or dishes, sending letters, or food preparation. Discuss how scientific achievements have affected our way of living.

Recommended Books

Avi. *Night Journeys.* New York: Pantheon, 1979.

Beatty, Patricia. *Be Ever Hopeful, Hannalee.* New York: Morrow, 1988.

Beatty, Patricia. *Turn Homeward, Hannalee.* New York: Morrow, 1984.

Blumberg, Rhoda. *The Incredible Journey of Lewis and Clark.* New York: Lothrop, 1987.

Kimmel, Eric A. *Charlie Drives the Stage.* New York: Holiday, 1989.

Lord, Betty B. *In the Year of the Boar and Jackie Robinson.* New York: Harper & Row, 1986.

Talbot, Charlene. *Orphan for Nebraska.* New York: Atheneum, 1979.

Contributions (research, illustrative reporting)

42

Help the students construct geometric designs, leaving an open space in the center. From the center space, draw lines connecting to smaller shapes outside of the geometric design. Then have students print the name of a group being studied in the center space. Ask them to fill in the smaller spaces with pictures representing the groups' contributions to civilization. Suggest that students color the background of each space a different color and outline each with a marker to make an eye-catching design.

Recommended Books

Beard, Annie. *Our Foreign-Born Citizens.* New York: Crowell, 1968.

Behrens, June. *Fiesta! Ethnic Traditional Holidays.* Chicago: Childrens Press, 1978.

De Paola, Tomie. *An Early American Christmas.* New York: Holiday, 1987.

Dobler, Lavinia. *Customs and Holidays Around the World.* New York: Fleet, 1962.

Forest, Heather. *The Baker's Dozen: A Colonial American Tale.* San Diego: Harcourt Brace Jovanovich, 1988.

Hanmer, Trudy. *Haiti.* New York: Watts, 1988.

Hayes, Sarah. *Away in the Manger.* New York: Simon & Schuster, 1987.

Kismaric, Carole. *The Rumor of Pavel and Paali: A Ukrainian Folktale.* New York: Harper & Row, 1988.

Silverman, Maida. *Festival of Lights: The Story of Hanukkah.* New York: Wanderer, 1987.

43

Create a History (creative writing, research)
If possible, collect old photographs, magazines, and calendars. Have children select pictures of a person, place, or event and create historical descriptions of the pictures. Encourage students to look at the clothing worn and any identifiable objects in the background or scenery.

44

Current Events (interpretative reading, oral reporting)
Set aside a special weekly time to share news items related to the area of study. Ask students to listen to the nightly news and skim the daily paper to gain information. If news is scarce, encourage students to share interesting facts or stories about the place or period of study.

45

A Debate (research, critical thinking, oral expression)
Help students plan a debate between historic persons who hold different viewpoints on one or more issues. Suggest that debaters need not be from the same time period or from the same place. Examples:
• Alexander Hamilton and Thomas Jefferson
• Queen Elizabeth I and King Philip of Spain
• Susan B. Anthony and a senator of her time
• Florence Nightingale and a representative of the British War Ministry
• Father Junipero Serra and the Viceroy of Spain concerning the purposes of the Spanish missions in

California
- Columbus versus Ferdinand of Spain
- Thomas Paine versus George III
- William Seward versus opposing senators on the Alaska Purchase
- Elizabeth Blackwell and the head of a medical school
- Roger Williams and a Puritan leader on religious freedom
- Captain John Smith and Powhatan

Design a Castle (reference, research, illustrative reporting)
Have students research and design castles that would be

46

typical of a period or area. Ask students to write descriptions and rationales for the type of construction. If time allows and materials are available, encourage students to build models of their castles. Have students compare their castles with castles of other areas.
Examples:
- Welsh with English
- German with English
- Spanish with French

Recommended Books

De Angeli, Marguerite. *The Door in the Wall*. New York: Scholastic, 1984.
Eager, Edward. *Knight's Castle*. San Diego: Harcourt Brace Jovanovich, 1965.
Macaulay, David. *Castle*. Boston: Houghton Mifflin, 1977.
Pyle, Howard. *Men of Iron*. Mahwah, NJ: Troll, 1989.

Rutland, Jonathan. *Knights and Castles.* New York: Random House, 1987.

Smith, Beth. *Castles.* New York: Watts, 1988.

Winthrop, Elizabeth. *The Castle in the Attic.* New York: Holiday, 1985.

47

Defense Argument (research, critical thinking, oral expression)

Suggest that students prepare arguments in defense of controversial subjects. Encourage students to present their arguments orally. Remind students that arguments should be supported by good reference and research work. A question and answer period might follow the presentations. Examples:

- hydraulic mining
- slavery
- fur trapping
- Louisiana Purchase
- building the Suez Canal
- Boston Tea Party
- purchase of Alaska
- exploration of the New World
- French Revolution

48

A Documentary Drama (research, creative writing, dramatic expression)

Help the class stage a documentary drama of a historic event. Have students work in small groups to develop a script, devise costumes, collect props, select music, and decide on the casting. Sometimes forming a choral-speaking group to back up a speaker creates a dramatic effect. Present the documentary drama to another class, the whole school, or a community group.

49

Election Activity (research)

Hold a classroom election. Select subjects that children will be interested in. Some examples might be the most exciting dinosaur, most lovable pet, or most important school subject. Allow a given time for children to make choices and campaign. Help children set up campaign headquarters for each candidate. Have children make posters and buttons for the candidates. Balloons might be decorated with magic markers, then blown up to display messages. Help children make effective campaign slogans. Use study carrels or appliance cartons as voting booths. Ballot boxes might be made out of shoeboxes. Ask a group of children to tally the votes and announce the official winner. Arrange to take the class to see actual voting polls on election day, if possible.

Recommended Book

Archer, Jules. *Winners and Losers: How Elections Work in America*. San Diego: Harcourt Brace Jovanovich, 1984.

50

Energy (research, reporting, drawing conclusions)
To extend a unit on energy, have students calculate the cost of operating home appliances. Ask students to list all the electrical appliances in their homes. If possible, invite an electric company representative to come speak to the class. Obtain the figures needed to calculate the cost of operating each appliance for one week. With the class, brainstorm ways to reduce electrical use. For example, towel-dry hair, use wind-up clocks, and hang towels on the clothesline. Ask students, with their parents' help, to save as much energy as possible for one week. Suggest that students keep a written record of their efforts. Hold a class discussion at the end of the week. Using the figures from the electric company, see how much energy and money the entire class has saved. Help students draw conclusions about the economic value of saving energy.

Recommended Books

Berger, Melvin. *Energy from the Sun*. New York: Crowell, 1976.
Branley, Franklyn. *Energy for the 21st Century*. New York: Crowell, 1975.
Douglas, John H. *The Future World of Energy*. New York: Watts, 1984.

51

Environmental Effects (critical thinking, drawing conclusions)
Help students list ways the environment has affected

the development of this country. Next, list how the environment affects the students' daily living. A third list might show how the environment affects people in other countries. Help students draw conclusions concerning influences of the physical environment on civilization and which influences are greatest, least, positive, and negative. Conclusions might be compiled into a class chart. An extension of this project might be a study of humanity's abuse of the physical environment and the results of this abuse.

Recommended Books

Allen, Thomas B. *Where the Children Live.* Englewood Cliffs, NJ: Prentice Hall, 1980.

Bellamy, David. *Our Changing World: The Forest.* Southbridge, MA: Crown, 1988.

Bellamy, David. *Our Changing World: The River.* Southbridge, MA: Crown, 1988.

Lampton, Christopher. *Endangered Species.* New York: Watts, 1988.

Environmental Skits (critical thinking, dramatic expression)

52 Have students document the ways a society is regulated by its immediate environment. Encourage students to create skits to demonstrate the impact of one's natural surroundings.

Environmental Talks (research, reporting, oral expression)

Ask students to imagine they are citizens of the country being studied and that the citizens are asked by a group of natural scientists from another **53** country to discuss the impact of the environment on human life. The group would like the citizens to describe how the surroundings, climate, and land location affect daily living and business in the country. Ask students to assume the role of one of the following:

- New England farmer
- plantation owner
- rice farmer in China
- collective farmer in Russia
- vintner in France
- grain farmer in Iowa

54

Events Comparison (illustrative interpretation, research)
Help students create a timeline for a specific time period. Have the students research events that occurred in different parts of the world during the same time period. Encourage students to illustrate the dates. Help students draw conclusions by comparing the events from different countries.

55

Expanding Vocabulary (vocabulary, research)
As a way to expand students' vocabulary, hang several sheets of paper on the wall labeled "Early Times," "Medieval Times," and "Early Modern Times." As students read historical novels, have them jot down words appropriate to that era. Later, have students add the words to the lists on the wall. Ask students to research the meanings of the words and explain the words to the class. A certain time might be set aside to introduce the new words to the class.

56

Exploration (research, notetaking, reporting)
As a class, select an area of land that includes various land formations and forms of plant and animal life. Ask students to imagine that they are exploring the area for the first time. Discuss why it is important to be accurate and observant while exploring. Have children draw maps and take detailed notes as they explore the area. Ask the students to submit final reports to the class for discussion.

57

Explorer Dialogue (selecting pertinent facts, creative writing)
Ask the class to imagine a dialogue between two explorers whose territories or experiences are similar. Each wishes to impress the other with the dangers and

Columbus

Magellan

hardships of his or her own expedition. The explorers also want to describe the new and exciting things they have seen and done. Arrange the class into groups of two. Ask the groups to research and write a dialogue between two explorers. Encourage the groups to present their dialogues to the rest of the class. Dialogues might be between:

- De Soto and Balboa
- Columbus and Magellan
- Richard Byrd and Roald Amundsen
- Meriwether Lewis and Marco Polo
- Sally Ride and Yuri Gagarin

Extend the Dialogue (creative writing)
Have the class read several historical novels or short stories. Then ask students to choose a particular dialogue and explain how it might be made into a skit or short play. Encourage the students to think about the following questions. What else might the characters have said? What might have happened the night before or the day after? What were the characters thinking about? Then arrange the class into small groups. Have the groups extend dialogues between historical characters from a particular scene in a story or novel.

58

Recommended Books

Coerr, Eleanor. *Chang's Paper Pony*. New York: Harper & Row, 1988.

Gates, Doris. *Blue Willow*. New York: Penguin, 1940.

Greene, Bette. *Summer of My German Soldier*. New York: Bantam, 1984.

Snyder, Zilpha. *The Egypt Game*. New York: Dell, 1986.

Speare, Elizabeth. *Calico Captive*. Boston: Houghton Mifflin, 1957.

Szilagyi, Mary. *Adventures of Charlie and His Wheat-Straw Hat.*
New York: Putnam, 1986.
White, T. H. *The Sword in the Stone.* New York: Dell, 1978.

Fact or Inference (critical thinking)
Have students select newspaper articles about people. Ask the students to underline the statements that are facts with one line and statements that are inferences with two lines. Have students share the results with others.

59

Farm Display (illustrative reporting, research)

Rooster

Pig

Goat

60

Help the class prepare an exhibit of "Farm Animals Around the World" or "Farm Machines Around the World." Have students research and write brief descriptions of farm animals or machinery. Exhibits may consist of pictures, cutouts, clay or toy animals, mockups, or models. As an extension of this activity, other exhibits may be developed, such as "Costumes Around the World," "Transportation Around the World," or "Flowers Around the World."

A Farm Fair (research, critical thinking, oral expression)
Plan a Farm Fair where students become farmers from different regions or countries. Have students research the crops, animals, farm problems, and farming methods of specific regions. Costumes or parts of costumes may be worn by the participants to enhance the presentation. Have the student-farmers prepare some questions to ask their fellow farmers from other places. Then have the farmers mingle to allow time for their questions. At the close of the fair, have the student-farmers write reports to their various farm organizations sharing what they learned at the fair.

61

Recommended Books

Anderson, George. *The American Family Farm*. San Diego: Harcourt Brace Jovanich, 1989.

Bellville, Cheryl W. *Farming Today Yesterday's Way*. Minneapolis: Carolrhoda, 1984.

Demuth, Patricia. *Joel: Growing Up a Farm Man*. New York: Putnam, 1982.

Marston, Hope I. *Machines on the Farm*. New York: Putnam, 1982.

McManigal, J.W. *Farm Town*. Lexington, MA: Stephen Greene, 1987.

62

Float Parade (illustrative reporting, art)
Suggest that the class watch the Pasadena Tournament of Roses on New Year's Day, Macy's Thanksgiving Day Parade, a local Veterans Day Parade, or other similar parades to introduce a float-making activity. Themes for floats may be geographical, historical, or biographical. The floats may center around books of fiction or nonfiction as well. A parade of floats representing various regions of the country may be used as a culmination to a unit or theme. Have children use shoeboxes as the base for a miniature float. Materials that might be used include construction paper, tissue paper, colored napkins, chicken wire, and cardboard.

Recommended Book

Fenten, Barbara and Fenten, D.X. *The Team Behind the Great Parades*. Louisville, KY: Westminster, 1981.

63

Food Sources (research, reporting)
Ask children to bring empty food containers, box tops, and labels to school. Then have children use magazines and seed catalogs to find pictures of the plants from which the food was derived. Make a display of the food containers and pictures. Ask the students to write brief descriptions of the various foods. Students might include explanations of the processing of the raw food and the nutritional value of the foods. Encourage children to indicate the foods they like best and compare their choices.

Recommended Books

Perl, Lila. *Hunter's Stew and Hangtown Fry*. Merlin, OR: Clarion, 1979.

Perl, Lila. *Slumps, Grunts, and Snickerdoodles: What Colonial America Ate and Why.* Merlin, OR: Clarion, 1979.

Foods Around the World (research)

64

Help the class collect pictures, box tops, cartons, and can labels that represent foods introduced by immigrants. Make a bulletin-board and table display of the food containers collected. Invite parents, relatives, or friends to send samples of their native foods to school for the class to sample. Ask parents to include a description of the food, special uses, the preparation, and its historical significance, if possible. Some may be willing to demonstrate food preparation for the class, followed by a tasting session.

Recommended Book

Hayward, Ruth A. and Warner, Margaret B. *What's Cooking? Favorite Recipes from Around the World.* Boston: Little, Brown, 1981.

Forts of Long Ago (research, illustrative reporting)

65

Help the class study the role of forts in the advancement of people moving from the east to the west in both the Old World and the New World. Start with an article from an encyclopedia. Help students identify the names of important forts that were built in Europe and North America. Investigate forts built by French, English, Spanish, and Americans in North America as well. Suggest that some students research the weaponry of the various periods or the political importance of each fort. Have students summarize their research by writing and illustrating their information for the class.

Recommended Book

Giblin, James. *Walls: Defenses Throughout History.* Boston: Little, Brown, 1984.

Historical and Political Cartoons (creative thinking)

66

Set aside bulletin-board space for historical and political cartoons. Display a few cartoons and discuss their humorous and satirical intent, as well as their uses. Ask students to bring cartoons to share with the class. As each new cartoon is added to the collection, ask the collector to explain its meaning, if possible. Once students become familiar with the cartoon genre, encourage them to create cartoons of their own.

Historical Couplets (creative poetry, art)
Read rhymed couplets to the class. Have students compose poems using the rhymed couplet form about historic events, people, or characters from historical novels. Have the students print the poems on drawing paper and decorate the borders with designs or pictures appropriate for the time.

67

Historic Greats (research, critical thinking)
Discuss the meaning of greatness with the class. Make a list on the chalkboard of historic greats. A few historic greats include Marie Curie, Louis Pasteur, Albert Schweitzer, Jane Addams, and Martin Luther King, Jr. In one comprehensive paragraph, have students prove that a historic person was great. Remind students that greatness is the cumulative result of what a person is or has done, rather than the result of a single deed.

68

Historical Interview (reference, research, speaking)
Arrange an interview with a historical character. Ask a parent, principal, or fellow teacher to assume the role of a historical character. Both the interviewer and the historical character will need to become familiar with the selected character's life, achievements, and opinions. Have the class prepare questions for the interviewer to ask. Ask for a volunteer or several volunteers to act as interviewers. An interesting program might be planned with several historical characters and interviewers.

69

BENJAMIN FRANKLIN 1776

70

Historical Radio Scripts (research, creative writing, speaking)

Discuss radio dramatization with the class. If possible, have students listen to a radio script. Then have students write radio scripts based on historical novels or on actual historic events. Suggest that they add music and sound effects. Record the scripts on tape for future listening.

Recommended Books

Baker, Betty. *Walk the World's Rim.* New York: Harper & Row, 1965.

Coerr, Eleanor. *Chang's Paper Pony.* New York: Harper & Row, 1988.

Fleischman, Sid. *By the Great Horn Spoon.* Boston: Little, Brown, 1963.

Fritz, Jean. *Early Thunder.* New York: Coward, 1967.

Kelly, Eric P. *The Trumpeter of Krakow.* New York: Macmillan, 1966.

O'Dell, Scott. *The Captive.* Boston: Houghton Mifflin, 1979.

Pierce, Tamora. *Alanna: The First Adventure.* New York: Dell, 1978.

Warski, Maureen C. *A Boat to Nowhere.* Louisville, KY: Westminster, 1980.

Historical Riddles (creative thinking, creative, writing, speaking)

71

Help students compose riddles related to historic events or characters from a historical novel. Or use reference materials to identify Mother Goose rhymes that refer to historical figures. Discuss with the students the underlying meaning of the rhymes. Using examples from Mother Goose, encourage students to write their own riddles. Before the activity, it might be helpful to establish some rules. For example, establish the number of clues given, with the first clue being difficult and succeeding clues easier. Encourage students to present their riddles orally. They may enjoy researching costumes and customs of their characters' time and wear appropriate clothing items when presenting.

Recommended Books

Adler, David. *Remember Betsy Floss and Other Colonial American Riddles*. New York: Bantam, 1989.

Keller, Charles and Baker, Richard. *The Star-Spangled Banana: And Other Revolutionary Riddles*. Englewood Cliffs, NJ: Prentice Hall, 1974.

72

Historical Scripts (research, creative writing, dramatic expression)
Have students write scripts dramatizing historical scenes. Examples:

- Boston Tea Party
- Lincoln's assassination
- signing of the Declaration of Independence
- Unification of Germany
- Columbus at the court of Isabella
- Nelson Mandela's release from prison
- Roger Williams and the Narragansett Indians
- Francis Scott Key writing "The Star Spangled Banner"
- Robert E. Lee surrendering to Ulysses S. Grant

73

Historical Vacations (research, comparing and contrasting)
Have students plan vacations in a given historical year. For example, what kind of vacation would someone have in 1890? Encourage students to emphasize the differences with vacationing today. Or suggest that students become a historical character and plan a vacation for him or herself. Remind students to consider their character's interests and means of travel.

74

A House of Representatives (research, notetaking, oral expression)
Help students dramatize the House of Representatives in the process of passing a bill. Have participants draw lots for their political parties, their positions on the bill (for or against), the state they represent, and the role of the Speaker of the House. The bill should be of interest

to the students. If possible, follow the United States Congress procedures. Allow time for delegates to plan strategies and caucuses with other delegates. Point out the importance of detailed and careful preparation and organization. A similar type of activity may be planned for meetings of the United Nations, Organization of American States, or the Common Market nations. Representatives might meet to discuss a particular agenda or consider problems in areas of economics, urbanization, agriculture, or other appropriate issues.

75

Houses of Worship (research, visual reporting)
Have students draw or collect pictures of various houses of worship. Encourage students to describe the types of architecture, various rooms or sections of the buildings, and the building's relationship to the specific religion. As an extension, suggest that groups of students research the different religious beliefs and compare their findings.

76

Important Books (reporting, creative writing)
Read *The Important Book* by Margaret Wise Brown to the children. In a group, discuss subjects important to the students. Examples might be the classroom guinea pig, school picture day, or rain at recess. Then talk about what is important individually. Ideas include families, pets, friends, and activities. As a class, make an "Important Book" for the classroom. Have children write and illustrate what is important to them. Compile all the writings and illustrations into a class booklet. Older students might use this form of importance for simple reports. Reports might include animals, weather phenomena, or machines. Help students discriminate between personal and factual choices.

Recommended Book

Brown, Margaret Wise. *The Important Book*. New York: Harper & Row, 1984.

77

Imported Customs (research, reporting)

With the class, study customs of the different immigrant cultures. Some customs include Christmas trees, Easter eggs, menorahs, piñatas, and valentines. Help the children design a bulletin-board display of drawings, pictures, and written stories or descriptions of holiday customs. Invite representatives of various countries to come speak to the class.

Recommended Books

Ashabranner, Brent. *The New Americans*. New York: Putnam, 1983.

Barth, Edna. *A Christmas Feast: Poems, Sayings, Greetings, and Wishes*. Merlin, OR: Clarion, 1979.

Barth, Edna. *Hearts, Cupids, and Red Roses*. Merlin, OR: Clarion, 1982.

Barth, Edna. *Holly, Reindeer, and Colored Lights: The Story of the Christmas Symbols*. Merlin, OR: Clarion, 1985.

Barth, Edna. *Lilies, Rabbits, and Painted Eggs: The Story of the Easter Symbols*. Merlin, OR: Clarion, 1981.

Barth, Edna. *Shamrocks, Harps, and Shillelaghs: The Story of the St. Patrick's Day Symbols*. Merlin, OR: Clarion, 1982.

Barth, Edna. *Turkeys, Pilgrims, and Indian Corn: The Story of the Thanksgiving Symbols*. Merlin, OR: Clarion, 1979.

Bernstein, Joanne E. *Dmitry: A Young Soviet Immigrant*. Merlin, OR: Clarion, 1981.

Cohen, Barbara. *Molly's Pilgrim*. New York: Lothrop, 1983.

Fisher, Leonard E. *Ellis Island: Gateway to the New World*. New York: Holiday, 1986.

Freedman, Russell. *Immigrant Kids*. New York: E. P. Dutton, 1980.

Kismaric, Carole. *The Rumor of Pavel and Paali: A Ukrainian Folktale*. New York: Harper & Row, 1988.

Levinson, Riki. *Watch the Stars Come Out*. New York: Macmillan, 1987.

Meltzer, Milton. *The Chinese Americans*. New York: Crowell, 1980.

78

Imported Goods (research, illustrative reporting, drawing conclusions)

With the class, collect advertisements and articles about imported goods from other countries. Mount the advertisements and articles on a bulletin board. Use this as background for a display of some actual imported items from grocery and department stores. Ask students to study the display and draw conclusions regarding the types, sources, and amounts of goods imported by the countries they have chosen. In small groups or as a class, share the individual conclusions and develop summarizing statements. As an extension activity, ask groups of students to prepare a similar bulletin board as it might be developed by a teacher in another country. Repeat the individual conclusions and summarizing statement activity.

Imported Tales (creative writing)

79 Ask children to trace the journey of an imported object. Examples might include a teakwood table from Japan, a madras shirt from India, or an opal ring from Australia. Have students write the history of the object, including the origin, development, and the trip to another country. Suggest that students illustrate the narration with stick figures or line drawings.

International Student News Correspondents (research, newswriting)

80 Have students become correspondents for a class International Student Newspaper. Encourage students to make press badges with the lettering "ISNC," their name, and the country each correspondent represents. Ask for volunteers to become the editorial board of the newspaper. Editorial board responsibilities might include editing, organizing, and printing the paper. Correspondents will submit student news items to the board. Articles might be about school, sports, work, recreation, or home life. It might be a good idea to set deadlines for each issue, as on a regular newspaper.

Recommended Books

Burnstein, Chaya M. *The Jewish Kids Catalog.* Philadelphia: Jewish Publication Society, 1983.

Watson, Jane W. *India Celebrates.* Champaign, IL: Garrard, 1974.

Watson, Jane W. *Parade of Soviet Holidays.* Champaign, IL: Garrard, 1974.

Watson, Tom and Watson, Jenny. *Evening Meal.* Chicago: Childrens Press, 1983.

Watson, Tom and Watson, Jenny. *Midday Meal.* Chicago: Childrens Press, 1983.

Wyndham, Lee. *Holidays in Scandinavia.* Chicago: Childrens Press, 1975.

I Search (research)

81

This activity encourages students to see themselves as a part of the research process. Help students choose topics of interest. In primary grades, the entire group might work on related material. Have the children work from three lists: "What I Already Know," "What I Would Like to Learn," and "What I Have Learned." Help students list what they already know on one sheet of paper and questions they have about the topic on a second sheet. A third sheet of paper will be needed to answer their questions. Have children research their topics using library and classroom books. Ask children to make notes on the third sheet, answering as many of their own questions as possible. Help students arrange their information into reporting form. Older students may enjoy researching topics in which they have a personal interest. Have students include the reasons for their interest, experiences in learning about the topic, and plans for future learning. Example:

> I have always enjoyed hiking. Now that I am old enough to take longer trips, I need to buy some good hiking boots. I've decided to look for information about how hiking boots are made and how to choose the best pair for the different types of trails. At the sporting goods store, I examined boots and learned . . .

A Jeweler's Visit (notetaking)

82

Invite a local jeweler to visit the class for a discussion of precious and semi-precious stones. Encourage the class to create an invitation to be delivered by class members. The invitation might explain that gems are important products of a region being studied or a current topic in their science class. Encourage

students to take notes while the jeweler is speaking. Following the event, have the students write a paragraph summarizing the material covered. As an extension, have children locate gem deposits on a world map, learn the processes of mining, refining the stones, or the metals used in making settings. Stories of famous gems, such as the Hope diamond, may also be found and reported on. Interested students might wish to design their own jewelry as well.

Lawmaking (research, reporting, critical thinking)
As a class activity, draw a chart showing the steps in enacting a federal law. Assign groups of students to find out whether city, county, and state laws and ordinances are enacted in the same way. Have the groups report their findings to the class. Encourage the groups to make additional charts showing local, county, and state processes as well. Have students study the charts to prepare for a general discussion. Suggest that students list what they believe to be the reasons for the differences, as well as the advantages and disadvantages of the different processes.

83

Letter from a Leader (research, creative writing)
Have the students compose a letter as it might have been written by the leader of an exploration, colony, or country. Encourage students to describe the difficulties and rewards of a high position. The letter might be written to a friend or relative of the chosen leader. Some people that might be selected include:

84

• Governor John Winthrop of Massachusetts Bay
  Colony
• Sir Walter Raleigh
• Queen Elizabeth
• Benito Juarez
• Margaret Thatcher
• Robert E. Lee
• John F. Kennedy
• Meriwether Lewis or William Clark
• Nelson Mandela
• William Penn
• Marco Polo
• Julius Caesar
• Amelia Earhart

A Letter Home (research, creative writing)

Have students choose an important moment in the life of a historical character and write a letter home from the character. Remind students to include the time, place, and events, as well as personal

85 thoughts and reasons for writing the letter. Examples:

- Daniel Boone
- Leif Ericson
- Malcolm X
- Pilgrim at Plymouth
- Pocahontas during her stay in England
- Marco Polo crossing Asia or imprisoned in Genoa
- Harriet Tubman
- Alexander somewhere in Egypt
- Florence Nightingale writing home from the Crimea

License Plates (creative thinking)

Ask children to suggest six-letter personalized license plates for states or countries being studied, such as

86 Alaska: B-R-R-R-R-R or C-O-O-O-O-L. Using construction paper or cardboard, have the students construct their own license plates describing a region or subject being studied.

Likeness (literature, critical thinking)

After reading historical novels, ask students to make a

87 list of items or processes that are similar today to the items or processes found in the historical novel. Discuss why the items or processes have remained the same.

Recommended Books

Beatty, Jerome. *The Tunnel to Yesterday*. New York: Avon, 1983.

Clapp, Patricia. *The Tamarack Tree*. New York: Lothrop, 1986.

Dalgliesh, Alice. *The Courage of Sarah Noble*. New York: Macmillan, 1986.

Dillon, Eilis. *The Seekers*. New York: Macmillan, 1986.

Gray, Elizabeth J. *Adam of the Road*. New York: Penguin, 1987.

Klaveness, Jan O. *The Griffin Legacy*. New York: Dell, 1985.

Levinson, Nancy S. *Clara and the Bookwagon*. New York: Harper & Row, 1988.

Speare, Elizabeth G. *The Sign of the Beaver*. Boston: Houghton Mifflin, 1983.

Wilder, Laura Ingalls. *Little House in the Big Woods*. New York: Harper & Row, 1953.

88

A Live Dinosaur (creative thinking)
Ask children to pretend to be a prehistoric animal that has come to life. Then have children share some of the events that happened to them and their impressions of the world today.

Recommended Books

Aliki. *Digging Up Dinosaurs*. New York: Crowell, 1988.

Aliki. *My Visit to the Dinosaurs*. New York: Crowell, 1985.

Aliki. *Wild and Woolly Mammoths*. New York: Crowell, 1977.

Arnold, Caroline. *Graveyard of the Past*. New York: Clarion, 1989.

Branley, Franklyn M. *Dinosaurs, Asteroids, and Superstars*. New York: Crowell, 1982.

British Museum. *Dinosaurs and Their Living Relatives*. Cambridge: Cambridge University, 1986.

Carrick, Carol. *Patrick's Dinosaurs*. Merlin, OR: Clarion, 1983.

Carrick, Carol. *What Happened to Patrick's Dinosaurs?* Merlin, OR: Clarion, 1986.

Cowley, Stewart. *The Mighty Giants*. New York: Warner, 1988.

Horner, John R. and Gorman, James. *Maia: A Dinosaur Grows Up*. Philadelphia: Running, 1987.

Lambert, David. *Dinosaur World*. New York: Macmillan, 1982.

Pringle, Laurence. *Dinosaurs and People: Fossils, Facts, and Fantasies*. San Diego: Harcourt Brace Jovanovich, 1978.

Sattler, Helen R. *Dinosaurs of North America*. New York: Lothrop, 1981.

89

Magazine Advertising (critical thinking)
With the class, discuss propaganda techniques used in advertising. Have students find three magazine advertisements. Ask students to cut and mount the advertisements on colored paper. Have students write a description of the propaganda techniques used in each advertisement. Then ask students to create an advertisement for another product, real or imaginary. Again, have

students write an explanation of the selling strategy used in their advertisements. Make a bulletin-board display of the advertisements and descriptions.

Magazine Article (composition)

Suggest that students write an article for a magazine about a historic event, a political incident, or a social situation. Remind students that magazine writers often include comments and opinions. Before writing the article, suggest that students decide who the audience will be for the magazine. Remind students to select incidents, details, and vocabulary to fit the audience.

90

Making Chants (poetry writing)

Ask children, individually, to repeat their names several times while the class claps softly to establish a rhythm. For example, "Johnny Brown" contains three syllables or beats and "Ann Smith" contains only two syllables or beats. Have children compose lines in a similar pattern. (Names serve to establish a rhythm, the chant need not be about the person.)

91

Johnny Brown	Ann Smith
Sun and moon	Dark cloud
Shine on me	Drop rain
Bring me light	On these
Show my way.	Parched fields.

Manufactured Goods (research, reporting)

As a group, make an inventory of manufactured goods found in the classroom. List the items on the chalkboard. Then list the raw materials and the name and location of the manufacturer. Keep the chart for several days, filling in information as it is located. When the chart is complete, begin a discussion to help students

92

draw conclusions from the data. Possible conclusions might be that almost everything used in our daily living is factory manufactured or that many of our products are synthetic. Each of the conclusions drawn by the class may be the subject of further research.

Recommended Books

Arnow, Jan. *Louisville Slugger: The Making of a Baseball Bat.* New York: Pantheon, 1984.

Claypool, Jane. *Manufacturing.* New York: Watts, 1984.

Cobb, Vicki. *The Secret Life of School Supplies.* Philadelphia: Lippincott, 1981.

Cohen, Daniel. *The Last Hundred Years: Household Technology.* New York: McEvans, 1982.

Charles, Oz. *How Does Soda Get into a Bottle?* New York: Simon & Schuster, 1988.

Crump, David, J., ed. *How Things Are Made.* Washington, D.C.: National Geographic, 1983.

Limousin, Odile. *The Story of Paper.* Ossining, NY: Young Discovery Library, 1988.

Rogow, Zack. *Oranges.* New York: Watts, 1988.

Weil, Lisl. *New Clothes: What People Wore—From Cavemen to Astronauts.* New York: Atheneum, 1987.

Mapmaking (visual representation, following directions)

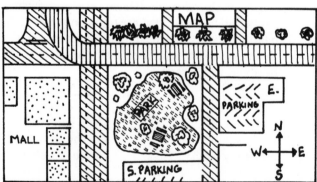

93

To sharpen map skills, invent a series of directions for drawing a map. Have students use drawing paper and pencils to sketch the map.
Example:

- Label the directions north, south, east, and west on the paper.

- A main highway runs north and south through the center of the map.
- The highway is bisected by one street running east and west in the middle of the map.
- The northeastern half of the map is a park. Label it.
- The entrance to the park is from a street that runs from east to west. Label the entrance.
- Draw three streets in the park that lead to a museum and picnic grounds, then out the north side.
- Name and label all streets and highways.

94

Mapping a Topic (research, illustrative reporting)
Help students use mapping to organize research projects. Suppose the class is interested in birds. Make a list of what students know about birds. Then make a second list of what they want to find out. Categorize questions on the list by asking which questions are related or belong together. Mark related questions with a similar symbol or color. Name each category. Then make a map with the birds' names or pictures in the center and categories written on the arms. Information can be recorded on the empty lines and paragraphs developed from the information on the arms. Have students use this process to research other topics of interest as well.

95

Matching Game (vocabulary)
Help students write words related to an area of study on cards. Write definitions or synonyms on the chalkboard or on a chart. The game may be played in teams or by individuals. Each team takes a turn drawing from the card pile and matching the cards with an item on the list. The team with the most correct matches wins. The game may be extended by asking students to add a fact about the word pair after making a correct match. Examples:
- De Soto—Mississippi River
- Balboa—Pacific Ocean
- Cortez—Peru
- Pizarro—Mexico
- Chief Sitting Bull—Battle of Wounded Knee
- Ponce de Leon—Florida
- Vasco da Gama—India
- Rosa Parks—desegregation

- King John—Magna Carta
- Robert Fulton—steamship
- Marie Curie—radium
- Clara Barton—Red Cross
- Alexander the Great—Macedonia
- Socrates—Athens

96

Meet the Press (research, critical thinking)
A "Meet the Press" program might be used for reference and research activities. Help students select a figure from history to interview. Ask for volunteers to be reporters for the Press Corps. Reporters will need to be familiar with details of the guest's life and work. Ask a student to represent the figure from history. This person, too, will need to be familiar with appropriate facts and details.

97

Methods Past and Present (creative writing)
After the class has studied a unit on agriculture, arrange the class into small groups. Ask the groups to write conversations between an elderly person and a young farmer comparing past farming methods with those used today. Ask students to discuss such topics as soil, weather, plant foods, types of plants, and insects. The activity might be extended to include methods of food preservation and marketing.

Recommended Books

Bellville, Cheryl W. *Farming Today Yesterday's Way.* Minneapolis: Carolrhoda, 1984.

Olney, Ross R. *The Farm Combine.* New York: Walker, 1984.

Patterson, Geoffrey. *Dairy Farming.* Bergenfield, NJ: Andre Deutsch, 1984.

Patterson, Geoffrey. *The Story of Hay.* Bergenfield, NJ: Andre Deutsch, 1983.

Rahn, Joan. *More Plants That Changed History.* New York: Atheneum, 1985.

Selsam, Millicent E. *Cotton.* New York: Morrow, 1982.

98

Modes of Travel (speaking, critical thinking)
Ask students who have traveled by car, boat, train, bus, or plane to talk about their various trips. Following the talks, help the class make lists of the advantages and disadvantages of each form of travel. Then ask students

to choose a destination and write a paragraph explaining their choice of transportation.

Morning Talk Show (planning, organizing, speaking, writing, reporting)
Use "Good Morning America," "Captain Kangaroo," and other television shows as models to help the class plan a talk show related to a current area of study. Help students select a theme song and decide on subjects for program segments. Subjects might include fashions, weather, recipes, music, or current events. Assign the segments to different groups of students. Help the class establish standards for timing, delivery, and clarity. Try taping the program and playing it back for the students. If the study extends over a length of time, more than one program might be developed.

99

Mosaic Monster (creative thinking, creative writing, art)

100

With the class, discuss a type of monster some of Columbus' crew might have imagined at the edge of the ocean. Provide students with large sheets of drawing paper and colored construction paper. Suggest that students tear the colored paper into pieces and glue them onto the drawing paper to make a mosaic-type monster. Have the children name their monsters and write a detailed description. Encourage the class to write about the sightings of the monster, too. Help the class make black frames for their monster portraits. Display the portraits on a bulletin board.

Recommended Books

Bulla, Clyde R. *My Friend the Monster*. New York: Crowell, 1980.
Kellogg, Steven. *Ralph's Secret Weapon*. New York: Dial, 1983.
Le Guin, Ursula K. *The Wizard of Earthsea*. Boston: Houghton Mifflin, 1968.
Meddaugh, Susan. *Too Many Monsters*. Boston: Houghton

Mifflin, 1982.

Selsam, Millicent E. *Sea Monsters of Long Ago.* New York: Four Winds, 1978.

Yep, Laurence. *Dragon of the Lost Sea.* New York: Harper & Row, 1988.

Yolen, Jane. *Dragons and Dreams.* New York: Harper & Row, 1986.

A Mural (illustrative reporting, art)

101 On a large sheet of butcher paper, have children create a mural depicting an event or scene from history. Suggest that students draw individual sketches on smaller paper and combine the ideas in a plan for the complete mural. Provide children with chalk or charcoal to rough in the outlines of their sketches. Have the class use tempera paint, colored chalk, and crayon to finalize the mural design. As a class, decide on a title.

JANUARY 24, 1848

My World (observation, research, reporting)

102 Give students pieces of string about two feet long with the ends tied together. Children will need pencil and paper to record their observations. Go outside to a grassy or woodsy area. Have the students choose an area to place their circle of string. Ask the children to observe the world within the circle for a few minutes. Suggest that children record the activities within the small world and speculate what is happening underneath. Encourage students to draw maps of the space. Then have children write a paragraph or story about what they observed.

Name Origins (research, reporting)

103 With the class, make a list of geographical names that have a known historical background. Ask students to research the names and write an explanation of the origin. Display results on a chart or bulletin board with space for additional entries. As different countries or areas are studied, encourage students to add them to the list. Examples:

• Washington, D.C.
• Lincoln, Nebraska
• Leesburg, Virginia
• Rome, Italy
• Alexandria, Egypt
• Lake Huron
• Death Valley

104

Narrative Poems (poetry writing)
Read to the class several narrative poems, such as "Paul Revere's Ride" by Henry Wadsworth Longfellow, "Columbus" by Joaquin Miller, "Hymn" by Ralph Waldo Emerson, and "Landing of the Pilgrim Fathers" by Felicia Hemans. Have students compose narrative poems about historic figures or favorite characters in historical novels. Encourage students to share their poems with the class.

Recommended Books

Blishen, Edward, ed. *Oxford Book of Poetry for Children.* New York: Oxford, 1987.
Longfellow, Henry Wadsworth. *Hiawatha.* New York: Dial, 1983.
Longfellow, Henry Wadsworth. *Paul Revere's Ride.*
 New York: Greenwillow Books, 1985.
Noyes, Alfred. *The Highwayman.* New York: Lothrop, 1983.

105

Native Festival (reference and research, visual reporting)
Hold a native festival for a country the class is studying. Help students research appropriate food, decorations, costumes, and dances. Ask for a volunteer to act as a Master of Ceremonies to coordinate the events. Plan a time to invite parents and relatives to the festival.

Recommended Books

Behrens, June. *Powwow.* Chicago: Childrens Press, 1983.
Hatch, Jane M., ed. *American Book of Days.* New York: Wilson, 1978.
Hopkins, Lee. *Do You Know What Day Tomorrow Is?* New York: Scholastic, 1990.

Perl, Lila and Ada, Alma F. *Piñatas and Paper Flowers—Piñatas y Flores de Papel: Holidays of the Americas in English and Spanish*. Merlin, OR: Clarion, 1985.

Watson, Jane W. *India Celebrates!* Champaign, IL: Garrard, 1974.

Watson, Jane W. *Parade of Soviet Holidays*. Champaign, IL: Garrard, 1974.

Wyndham, Lee. *Holidays in Scandinavia*. Champaign, IL: Garrard, 1975.

Native Food Content (research, reporting, critical thinking)

106

With the class, plan a food study of the region being studied. Ask students to research foods grown in the region and foods that are imported to that region. Encourage students to analyze the nutritional content of the major foods. If possible, invite a person from the region or one who has visited the region to come speak to the class about the native foods. Ask students to research the effects of the local diet on the people of the region.

Recommended Books

Ancona, George. *Bananas: From Manolo to Margie*. Merlin, OR: Clarion, 1982.

Peavy, Linda and Smith, Ursula. *Food, Nutrition, and You*. New York: Scribners, 1982.

Thompson, Paul. *Nutrition*. New York: Watts, 1981.

Watson, Tom and Watson, Jenny. *Evening Meal*. Chicago: Childrens Press, 1983.

Watson, Tom and Watson, Jenny. *Midday Meal*. Chicago: Childrens Press, 1983.

Natural Resources (research, illustrative reporting)

107

Help the class identify the natural resources of a continent, state, or country being studied. Ask children to find out how the resources are used. If possible, help identify the main trading countries for each of the resources. Encourage students to use world almanacs to learn the

monetary value of each resource. Create a bulletin-board display by having students draw pictures or collect magazine pictures of the natural resources. Encourage students to attach written statements about the resources to the illustrations.
Examples:

- metals
- lumber
- fish
- oil
- salt
- coal

108

A New Product (creative thinking, reporting)
Hold a class discussion about new products on the market. Also discuss the many steps involved in creating new products. Then ask students to create some new products. Have students name the product, create a company to manufacture it, and plan advertising for the product. Encourage students to write descriptions of their products as a part of this advertisement. Then ask students to act as salespersons for the companies and try to sell their products to the class.

Recommended Book

Campbell, Hannah. *Why Did They Name It*. New York: Fleet, 1964.

109

Newspaper Articles (creative writing)

Collect newspaper articles describing events that are happening in the world today. Share the articles with the class. Ask children to write a newspaper article describing an event in the history of the country being studied. Encourage students to imagine that they are at the scene and describe what is happening. Encourage students to give background information on the events, too. Examples:

- completion of the Panama Canal
- building Brasilia, the new capital of Brazil

- the founding of a new country in Africa
- beginning of the first session of the United Nations
- first successful trip of the Pony Express
- an event of the French Revolution
- the coronation of Napoleon

Newspaper Front Page (creative writing, research)
Share front pages of several newspapers with the class.
Then have students compose front pages of newspapers
describing an important historic event. Besides the lead
article, encourage students to write other articles for the
front page. As an extension, group students together
and give each group articles on the same subjects. Have
the groups use their articles to produce a special edition
newspaper.
Examples:

110

- end of the Civil War
- signing of the Declaration of Independence
- opening of the West
- gold is discovered in California or Alaska
- Julius Caesar becomes dictator of Rome
- 19th amendment passed
- Phillip of Macedonia dies
- Spanish Armada sets sail
- Phoenicians produce a new alphabet
- laws in Civil Rights Act of 1964 passed

Original Documents (creative thinking, research)

111

Locate copies of primary
documents for the class to
examine. Examples of
documents include the Magna
Carta, Declaration of Independence, Bill of Rights,
Declaration of the Rights of
Man and of the Citizen,
United Nations Charter, and
Louisiana Purchase. Help
students create charts to
compare likenesses and
differences of the documents
in purpose, content, language,
and effect on the history of
civilization. Encourage

students to learn where the original materials are kept and how the manuscripts are preserved.

Recommended Book

Carey, Helen and Greenberg, Judith. *How to Use Primary Sources.* New York: Watts, 1983.

112

Original Myths and Folktales (creative writing, art) Read aloud a few myths or folktales. Encourage children to read others on their own. Have the class write original myths or folktales that relate to the beliefs of the country and people being studied. Encourage students to illustrate the tales using materials and art forms appropriate for the culture. Written tales may be bound in a class book. Provide time for children to share their stories with the rest of the class, another group, or as a program for parents and guests.

Recommended Books

Coolidge, Olivia. *Greek Myths.* Boston: Houghton Mifflin, 1949.

D'Aulaire, Ingri and D'Aulaire, Edgar P. *D'Aulaires' Book of Greek Myths.* New York: Doubleday, 1980.

D'Aulaire, Ingri and D'Aulaire, Edgar P. *D'Aulaires' Norse Gods and Giants.* New York: Doubleday, 1986.

De Paola, Tomie. *The Lady of Guadalupe.* New York: Holiday, 1980.

De Paola, Tomie. *The Legend of the Indian Paintbrush.* New York: Putnam, 1987.

Goble, Paul. *Buffalo Woman.* New York: Bradbury, 1984.

Goble, Paul. *Gift of the Sacred Dog.* New York: Macmillan, 1984.

Goble, Paul. *Star Boy.* New York: Bradbury, 1983.

Guy, Rosa. *Mother Crocodile: An Uncle Amadou Tale from Senegal.* New York: Delacorte, 1982.

Hamilton, Virginia. *The People Could Fly.* New York: Knopf, 1985.

McDermott, Gerald. *Anansi the Spider: A Tale from the Ashanti.* New York: Holt, 1972.

McDermott, Gerald. *Arrow to the Sun: A Pueblo Indian Tale.* New York: Penguin, 1977.

McDermott, Gerald. *Daughter of the Earth: A Roman Myth.* New York: Delacorte, 1984.

McDermott, Gerald. *The Stonecutter: A Japanese Folk Tale.* New York: Penguin, 1975.

Perrault, Charles. *Puss in Boots.* Mahwah, NJ: Troll, 1979.

Shulevitz, Uri. *The Treasure.* New York: Farrar, Straus & Giroux, 1979.

Singer, Isaac Bashevis. *Mazel and Schlimazel Or the Milk of a Lioness.* New York: Farrar, Straus & Giroux, 1967.

Uchida, Yoshiko. *The Magic Listening Cap.* Fort Lauderdale: Creative Arts, 1987.

113

A Panel Discussion (research, critical thinking, speaking)

Help the class present a panel discussion related to an important issue. Have students act as representatives for both sides of the argument. For example, participants on a panel concerning "Suitable Treatment of the Land" might be an English visitor, a Spanish colonist, and an American colonist. Panel members will need to research the topic from the viewpoint of the person they represent. Select a moderator to lead the discussion and handle questions from the audience at the close of the presentation.

114

Peace Corps (research, creative thinking)

Discuss the Peace Corps with the class. Or invite a former Peace Corps volunteer to come speak to the class about the activities of the Peace Corps. Ask the class to imagine themselves as members of the Peace Corps assigned to an underdeveloped country. Explain that the goal of the group is to provide water for an arid farming region. Ask students to study books, pictures, and films on the subject. Then ask the students to construct a diagram and written explanation of their proposals to give to the local government for approval. Other plans might be created for a new school, a children's clinic, or other public institutions.

115

Pen Pals (letter writing)

Have children write to pen pals from different locations. Encourage the children to share the returning letters with the class. If possible, arrange for students to have pen pals in the state or country they are studying. Students will receive firsthand information and share opinions with a person in another setting as a result of this activity.

116

Phenomenon Newscast (research, reporting)

Suggest that students write a television newscast about

a scientist describing an eclipse, the appearance of a comet, or other natural phenomena. Have students prepare charts, diagrams, and illustrations to help viewers understand the presentation. Try videotaping the newscast to share with other classes.

Recommended Books

Branley, Franklyn M. *Eclipse: Darkness in Daytime*. New York: Crowell, 1988.

Fradin, Dennis B. *Disaster! Blizzards and Winter Weather*. Chicago: Childrens Press, 1983.

Lauber, Patricia. *Volcano: The Eruption and Healing of Mt. St. Helens*. New York: Bradbury, 1986.

Simon, Seymour. *Storms*. Southbridge, MA: Crown, 1989.

Simon, Seymour. *Volcanoes*. New York: Morrow, 1988.

117

A Picture Dictionary of Terms (vocabulary)
With the class, list some of the terms being studied on a large piece of tagboard. Encourage students to place pictures that illustrate the terms on the chart. The pictures should help with the comprehension of the word. The pictures might be cut from magazines or drawn and colored.

Recommended Book

Knowlton, Jack. *Geography from A to Z: A Picture Glossary*. New York: Crowell, 1988.

118

A Picture Map (research, illustrative reporting)
Use a picture map to display important crops, industries, flowers, imports, exports, landmarks, and movements of different cultures being studied. Display an outline map of the desired area on a wall or bulletin board. Have children mount small pictures to show the locations of the selected subjects. Pictures may be students' colored illustrations or cut from magazines.

Plan a City (research, critical and creative thinking)
A class or group of students may enjoy designing a city
of the future. Ask children to list the needs of the city
and develop a plan for meeting these needs. Have
students look at factors, such as water supplies, conflicting needs for land use, problems with power supplies, waste disposal, and diminishing wildlife areas. Parks, public buildings, streets, highways, and shopping areas should also be considered. Encourage students to

119 think about suburban living and the problems

that could arise—for example, the demands on highways, transportation systems, pressures on businesses
to move outside of the city, and the adverse effect on
downtown areas. If possible, invite a member of the
local planning commission to serve as a consultant.
Provide students with materials to construct their cities.
Materials that might be used are large sheets of paper,
cardboard, and modeling clay. When the city models are
complete, ask students to write brief explanations of
their cities. An alternative project might be to redesign
the local town or city to provide for the needs of today
and the future.

Recommended Books

Goodall, John S. *The Story of an English Village.* New York:
Macmillan, 1979.
Macaulay, David. *City: A Story of Roman Planning and
Construction.* Boston: Houghton Mifflin, 1983.

Plan a Trip (research, reporting)
With the class, discuss the planning involved in taking a
trip. Ask students to choose a place they would like to

120 visit. Then have students plan their trips. Provide
materials, such as travel books, maps, airline timetables,
rent-a-car brochures, bus and train schedules, and

vacation clothing advertisements. Encourage students to plan the trips in detail, including transportation, hotels, stopovers, meals, clothing, passports, if necessary, rate of exchange, and estimated costs. Ask volunteers to present their itineraries to the class. An alternate activity might be to ask students to plan a group trip. This might include destination, type of travel, stops to be made, sights to be seen, and other details. Provide younger children with travel material. List a number of sights on big printed tickets. As the children find the sights in the materials, have them punch their tickets. Encourage children to write a sentence about the sights on their tickets.

Recommended Books

Anno, Mitsumasa. *Anno's Britain.* New York: Philomel, 1985.
Anno, Mitsumasa. *Anno's Italy.* New York: Philomel, 1984.
Anno, Mitsumasa. *Anno's Journey.* New York: Philomel, 1981.
Anno, Mitsumasa. *Anno's U.S.A.* New York: Philomel, 1983.
Billout, Guy. *By Camel or by Car: A Look at Transportation.* Englewood Cliffs, NJ: Prentice Hall, 1983.
Griffiths, David. *Pop-Up of Paris.* New York: Tarquin, 1986.
Krementz, Jill. *A Visit to Washington, D.C.* New York: Scholastic, 1987.
Lye, Keith. *Take a Trip to Venezuela.* New York: Watts, 1988.
Rogers, Fred. *Going on an Airplane.* New York: Putnam, 1989.
Sasek, M. *This Is Washington, D.C.* New York: Macmillan, 1973.
Swan, Robert. *Destination: Antarctica.* New York: Scholastic, 1989.
Wild, Anne. *Pop-Up London.* New York: Parkwest, 1985.
Wolff, Ashley. *The Bells of London.* New York: Putnam, 1984.

121

Propaganda Techniques (critical thinking)
Discuss the various propaganda techniques used in advertising. Help students organize an exhibit of examples showing and explaining the techniques. Examples might include leaflets, posters, television, radio, and newspaper advertisements. Suggest that written descriptions be made to explain how the particular techniques have been used.

122

Radio Talk Show (creative thinking, writing, speaking)
Listen to, and then discuss, a radio talk show. Ask

groups of students to create radio talk shows. The show might be taped, broadcast live, presented in the classroom, or transmitted over the school PA system. A set of rules might be helpful as students prepare their radio shows. For example:

- Programs must be exactly 10 minutes in length.
- Commercials must be entertaining and imaginative.
- Dead air (a period of silence) will lose points for the production.
- Scripts must be written and timed ahead of airing.

123

Reading a Map (literature, illustrative reporting)
Display a large map of the world in the classroom. Have students keep track of story settings on the map. Encourage students to pin a small book facsimile showing the title and author on the appropriate country.

124

Reforestation Panel (research, speaking)
Provide the class with information on reforestation. Select a panel of students to discuss the topic of reforestation as the topic relates to the area of study. Ask the panel to discuss clear cutting versus selective harvesting and the effects of logging on the environment. Panel members will need to research the topics in terms of the viewpoints they represent. Appoint a chairperson to preside over the panel. Ask the chairperson to direct the question and answer session following the panel discussion. Information may be obtained from the U.S. Forest Service, various environmental groups, and the U.S. Departments of Agriculture and Commerce.

125

Relief Map (illustrative reporting, art)
Help students become familiar with the topography of a particular area by creating a relief map. Have groups of students sketch an outline map on heavy cardboard. Help students mold the different levels of the map with papier-mâché according to a contour map of the area. When the map is dry, have students paint the land masses and bodies of water with appropriate colors.

Suggest that students label the areas with small flags made from toothpicks and paper. Ask a volunteer to make a legend for the map.

Research Riddles (reference skills, research)
Prepare a bulletin-board display of five to ten riddles that require research. Provide reference materials for students. Each week, post new riddles. Provide answer sheets with the question number in the first column, space for the answer in the second column, and space for **126** the name of the reference and page number in the third column. Offer a prize for the winning researcher. At the end of the week, share the correct answers with the class. A few sample questions include:

• How many teaspoons in a tablespoon?
• How many legs does a fly have?
• What is the longest river in Africa?

Schools Elsewhere (research, critical thinking)
Discuss schools in other countries or in other time periods. With the help of the class, transform the classroom into a schoolroom of another time or place. **127** Try using costumes, reading and writing materials, lunch preparations, and other props to help create an appropriate effect. At the end of the experience, have students write descriptions of their day.

Scrapbook: Influences of the Past (research)
Discuss how ancient cultures have influenced our lives today. Have the class collect advertisements, labels, and other items affected by the past. For example, Atlas Tires and Mercury Delivery Service use the names of mythological characters. Make a scrapbook by mounting the items on **128** paper, allowing space for a brief description. Ask students to choose one item and write explanations of how today's use of terms has been derived from the past. An alternative activity may be a class bulletin board

containing the same information. A follow-up activity might be for students to create advertisements for imaginary products using historical references.

Series of Illustrations (research, illustrative reporting)
Discuss how changes have evolved in a particular area of study. Ask students to draw a series of illustrations showing the changes over a period of time in specific phases of civilization. A few examples include:

129

- growth of a mining settlement into a city
- farm machinery from past to present
- changing modes of transportation
- homes past and present
- ancient ships to nuclear-powered vessels
- schools yesterday and today

Series of Pictures (literature, art)
After the class has read some historical novels, discuss how the novels might be illustrated. Have students draw a series of pictures illustrating a historical story or novel. Ask the students to label the illustrations. Suggest that the title, a comment about the story, and the name of the author be added to the illustrations. Bind the illustrations together in book form. Title the book "Illustrations of Historical Novels."

130

Recommended Books

Anderson, Margaret. *Searching for Shona*. New York: Knopf, 1978.
Beatty, Patricia. *Charley Skedaddle*. New York: Morrow, 1987.
Brown, Drollene. *Sybil Rides for Independence*. Chicago: Whitman, 1985.
Bulla, Clyde R. *Charlie's House*. New York: Crowell, 1983.

Gardiner, John. *Stone Fox.* New York: Crowell, 1980.

Reit, Seymour. *Behind Rebel Lines: The Incredible Story of Emma Edmonds, Civil War Spy.* San Diego: Harcourt Brace Jovanovich, 1988.

Taylor, Theodore. *Cay.* New York: Doubleday, 1989.

Treece, Henry. *Viking's Dawn.* Chatham, NY: S. G. Phillips, 1956.

Wisler, G. Clifton. *This New Land.* New York: Walker, 1987.

131

A Series of Steps (illustrative reporting)
Discuss the development of a particular historic event. Have students draw a series of illustrations or make a roller movie showing the development of the event. This might be done by arranging the class into small groups with each group working on a different event. Suggest that a written account of the event's progress accompany the illustrations. A few events include:

• Revolutionary War
• execution of Nathan Hale
• history of the American flag
• sailing and defeat of the Spanish Armada
• French Revolution

132

A Sailing Ship's Log (creative writing)
Have students create a page from a log of a historically famous ship. Arrange the class into small groups to research the movements of a famous ship. Ask the groups to include the following information in the log entry—where the ship is going, the current location of the ship, and the purpose of the journey. Students might also include feelings about the prospects of the voyage, events that have occurred during the past 24 hours, and weather information. A few historic ships are:

• Nina
• Mayflower
• Golden Hind
• Victory
• Constitution or Old Ironsides

Recommended Book

Blumberg, Rhoda. *Commodore Perry in the Land of the Shogun.* New York: Lothrop, 1985.

133

Ship Comparison (research, comparison, visual reporting)
Provide research materials so that students may study shipbuilding. Ask students to find pictures or sketch illustrations to accompany a written description of the scientific principles of shipbuilding. Encourage students to show how construction of old vessels and new vessels follow the same principles as well.

134

A Short Story (creative writing)
Have students write short stories about a time period or country the class is currently studying. Ask students to exchange papers and read the stories for historical and geographical accuracy as well as true representation of customs and attitudes. Encourage students to revise their stories, if necessary.

135

A Simulated Author Interview (research, creative thinking, speaking)
Discuss the meaning of a simulated interview with the class. Arrange the class into groups of two students each. Choose one student to be the author and the other to be the interviewer. Students will need to become familiar with the author's books, views, attitudes, and events of his or her personal life. Interviewers will need to prepare questions based on the information available about the author. Allow time for the groups to practice their interviews. Have students present their interviews to the class. Encourage questions from the audience following each interview.

Recommended Books

Blair, Gwenda. *Laura Ingalls Wilder.* New York: Putnam, 1981.
Cleary, Beverly. *A Girl from Yamhill: A Memoir.* New York: Morrow, 1988.
Commire, Anne. *Something About the Author: Facts and Pictures About Contemporary Authors and Illustrators for Young People.* Detroit: Gale Research, 1983.
Commire, Anne. *Yesterday's Authors of Books for Children.* Detroit: Gale Research, 1978.
De Montreville, Doris and Crawford, Elizabeth D., eds. *Third Book of Junior Authors.* New York: Wilson, 1972.
De Montreville, Doris and Crawford, Elizabeth D., eds. *Fourth Book of Junior Authors.* New York: Wilson, 1978.

Fuller, Muriel, ed. *More Junior Authors*. New York: Wilson, 1963.
Holtze, Sally H. *Fifth Book of Junior Authors and Illustrators*.
  New York: Wilson, 1983.
Kunitz, Stanley J. and Haycraft, Howard. *Junior Book of Authors*.
  New York: Wilson, 1951.
Meigs, Cornelia. *Invincible Louisa*. Boston: Little, Brown, 1968.

Sing-Along (research, participation)

136

Collect songs from different regions of the country, from a historical time, or another country. Use the school music series and the school and public libraries as resources. Make transparencies of the words to share with the class. Ask students to use maps and globes to identify where the songs originate. Provide a large outline map of the region for the students to mark on. As an extension, have groups of children find stories from these same places. A collection of work songs or sea songs may be extended in a similar fashion.

137

Situational Influences (literature, critical thinking)
Have students read historical novels. Help students document the ways in which the political and social situations of the times influenced the leading characters in the stories. Ask students to share their information with the rest of the class.

Recommended Books

Allan, Mabel E. *Mills Down Below*. New York: Putnam, 1981.
Avi. *Night Journeys*. New York: Pantheon, 1979.
Collier, James and Collier, Christopher. *Jump Ship to Freedom*.
  New York: Delacorte, 1981.
Greene, Bette. *Summer of My German Soldier*. New York:
  Bantam, 1984.
Griese, Arnold. *The Wind Is Not a River*. New York: Harper &

Row, 1978.

Hansen, Joyce. *Which Way Freedom*. New York: Walker, 1986.

McDonald, Joyce. *Mail-Order Kid*. New York: Putnam, 1988.

Speare, Elizabeth G. *The Bronze Bow*. Boston: Houghton Mifflin, 1973.

Stolz, Mary. *Zekmet the Stone Carver: A Tale of Ancient Egypt*. San Diego: Harcourt Brace Jovanovich, 1988.

A Soliloquy (creative writing and speaking)

Discuss the meaning of the word *soliloquy* with the class. Have students choose a historical character and write a soliloquy that the person might have delivered. Suggest that the soliloquy reveal the character's thoughts on the eve of an important event in which the character takes

138 part. Examples might include Thomas Edison demonstrating an invention before a scientific forum, Harriet Tubman asking to become a conductor for the Underground Railroad, and Cochise trying to make peace with the United States Army. Encourage students to reveal both the personal hopes and fears of their characters.

Recommended Books

Johnson, Ann D. *The Value of Adventure: The Story of Sacagawea*. Danbury, CT: Grolier, 1980.

Johnson, Ann D. *The Value of Helping: The Story of Harriet Tubman*. Danbury, CT: Grolier, 1979.

Johnson, Ann D. *The Value of Leadership: The Story of Winston Churchill*. Danbury, CT: Grolier, 1986.

Johnson, Ann D. *The Value of Responsibility: The Story of Ralph Bunche*. Danbury, CT: Grolier, 1978.

Johnson, Ann D. *The Value of Truth and Trust: The Story of Cochise*. Danbury, CT: Grolier, 1977.

A Special Week (research, reporting, writing, speaking)

Designate a particular week to celebrate a chosen country or subject area. Throughout the week, use as many activities as possible to develop an in-depth study

139 of the area. Help the class decorate the room with items from the region. Provide related books, stories, poems, songs, and dances for the students. Have the children draw pictures, play games and see films and videotapes related to the area of study. Try highlighting current events about the region, too. Help children serve a typical meal and invite guest speakers familiar with the area to come speak to the class. On the final day, help the children plan a program summarizing the week's activities.

140

Tableaux (research, illustrative reporting)
Help students create a series of tableaux portraying important scenes from a historical period being studied. Suggest costumes and props that are representative of the times and significant to the interpretation of the scenes. Have students arrange narration and background music for each scene.

141

Television News Broadcast (research, organization, speaking)
As a class, plan a television news broadcast of an important historic event. Choose students to become spot reporters that give detailed descriptions of the action. Details might include descriptions of the settings, spectators, weather, and the situations leading to the event. Ask for a volunteer to act as an anchor person to coordinate the broadcast and give the closing summary. Examples of some historic events:

- Generals Lee and Grant at Appomattox
- the assassination of Lincoln
- the Wright brothers' first flight
- the Boston Tea Party
- the sailing of the Spanish Armada
- Martin Luther King, Jr.'s, "I Have a Dream" speech
- Florence Nightingale returning from the Crimea

142

A Tourist Guide (research, illustrative reporting, creative writing)
Collect tourist guides to share with the class. Ask students to notice how the guides are written and the kind of information they contain. Have groups of students create tourist guides for cities or places of interest related to the area of study. Or have students make

booklets for visitors in the local community. Call the booklet "The Ten Places in _____ That No One Should Miss," for example. Help children decide what visitors would need to know, such as the importance of the place, what can be seen and done there, hours of operation, and entrance or parking costs. When information is gathered, help the children plan a format and produce the booklet. If possible, share the booklet with the Chamber of Commerce, Visitors' Bureau, or other agencies in the community.

Transportation Changes (research, illustrative reporting, art)

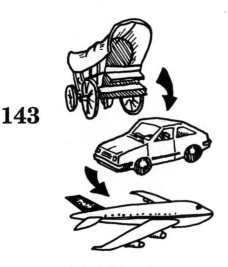

143

Help the class develop a frieze showing changes in transportation from early times to the present. Various types of transportation may be assigned to individual students and the pictures joined for the final frieze. Ask the artists to write explanations of the modes of transportation. Encourage students to draw and color the figures large enough for display. Friezes may be enhanced by the use of cut, colored paper.

Recommended Books

Jefferis, David. *Epic Flights*. New York: Watts, 1988.

Jefferis, David. *Giants of the Air: The Story of Commercial Aviation*. New York: Watts, 1988.

Lyon, David. *The Biggest Truck*. New York: Lothrop, 1988.

Marshall, Ray and Bradley, John. *The Car: Watch It Work by Operating the Moving Diagrams*. New York: Penguin, 1984.

McGowan, Alan and Van Der Meer, Ron. *Sailing Ships*. New York: Penguin, 1984.

McKissack, Patricia and McKissack, Frederick. *A Long, Hard Journey*. New York: Walker, 1989.

Tunis, Edwin. *Wheels: A Pictorial History*. New York: Harper & Row, 1977.

Wolverton, Ruth and Wolverton, Mike. *Trucks and Trucking*. New

York: Watts, 1982.

Zisfein, Melvin B. *Flight: A Panorama of Aviation.* New York: Knopf, 1981.

Trash Collection (research, reporting)

144 Encourage children to discuss the waste disposal problem by examining their own personal trash. Contact parents ahead of time and ask them to help their children collect a grocery bag of dry trash at home. On an appointed day, ask children to bring their trash to school. Discuss where to store the trash. Help the children see how their storage problem compares to the garbage disposal problems of a community. Help the children weigh their trash. Then have the children estimate the amount of trash for an entire community. Estimate the number of pounds, too. Have children sort their trash by type, such as newspaper, cardboard, plastic, and metal. Have the children weigh each type of trash. Discuss how trash is recycled, how people can reduce their amount of trash, and why some trash is more difficult to dispose of. If possible, have children take their trash to a local disposal site and become acquainted with the operation. Or invite a speaker to your classroom to answer questions about the problems of waste disposal and recycling in the community.

Recommended Books

Appelhof, Mary. *Worms Eat My Garbage.* Kalamazoo: Flower Press, 1982.

Simons, Robin. *Recyclopedia.* Boston: Houghton Mifflin, 1976.

Zion, Gene. *Dear Mr. Garbage Man.* New York: Harper & Row, 1988.

Travel Brochure (creative thinking, illustrative reporting)

145 Provide the class with travel brochures that advertise trips, tours, or special events. Then ask students to create illustrated travel brochures that advertise a historic voyage or expedition. Encourage students to vividly describe the new countries, animals, or people. Travel brochures might be about:

- a covered wagon train leaving for Oregon
- Marco Polo's venture to Cathay
- the Plymouth adventure

- the Crusades
- the Alaskan gold rush
- the New World to find the fountain of youth
- a French ship sailing for Canada
- Leif Ericson setting out for North America

Travel Rights (research, critical thinking, creative writing)

146 Ask the class to imagine being granted stage coach, railroad, or bus rights to a territory, state, or country. Have students draw routes to major cities or settlements and locate way stations for overnight stops and depots. Encourage students to research distances, types of terrain, rivers, and mountains to be crossed. Suggest that one group of students write a detailed description of the project to present to a government official of the region for approval.

Timeline (illustrative reporting)

147 Share several picture timelines with the class. Have students draw picture timelines to illustrate the sequence of events in historical novels. Remind students to select only the important events of the story to illustrate.

Recommended Books

Baker, Betty. *Walk the World's Rim.* New York: Harper & Row, 1965.

Bulla, Clyde R. *A Lion to Guard Us.* New York: Harper & Row, 1981.

Collier, James and Collier, Christopher. *Jump Ship to Freedom.* New York: Delacorte, 1981.

Flory, Jane. *The Great Bamboozlement.* Boston: Houghton Mifflin, 1982.

Forbes, Esther. *Johnny Tremain.* Boston: Houghton Mifflin, 1943.

Gray, Elizabeth J. *Adam of the Road.* New York: Penguin, 1987.

Hansen, Joyce. *Which Way Freedom.* New York: Walker, 1986.

Harvey, Brett. *Cassie's Journey: Going West in the 1860s.* New York: Holiday, 1987.

Hodges, Margaret. *The Avenger.* New York: Macmillan, 1982.

Keith, Harold. *Rifles for Watie.* New York: Harper & Row, 1957.

Levitin, Sonia. *No-Return Trail.* San Diego: Harcourt Brace Jovanovich, 1978.

Levitin, Sonia. *Roanoke*. New York: Macmillan, 1973.

Morrow, Honore. *On to Oregon*. New York: Morrow, 1946.

O'Dell, Scott. *Sarah Bishop*. Boston: Houghton Mifflin, 1980.

Page, Michael. *The Great Bullocky Race*. New York: Putnam, 1988.

Turner, Ann. *Nettie's Trip South*. New York: Macmillan, 1987.

148

Town Meeting (critical thinking, speaking)
Discuss the purpose of town meetings with the class. Help the class organize a town meeting at which a number of controversial issues are on the agenda. Assign roles to each class member. Have students carefully prepare arguments for and against the issues. Consult *Robert's Rules of Order* to help students learn how to conduct business at a public meeting.

149

Treasure Chest (research, reporting)
On a display table, arrange a collection of articles made from minerals used in modern industry. Have students dig for treasures by choosing objects from the treasure chest. Have the students identify the minerals used to manufacture the objects. Suggest that the findings be written and presented orally to the class.

150

Using a Data Chart (research, visual reporting)
Help the children develop research questions by asking, "What do we know about the topic?" and "What do we want to find out?" Prepare data charts for the class with spaces for recording appropriate information. Using the charts, have students make rough drafts of their reports, edit, and prepare a final version.

151

Venn Diagram Comparison (literature, making comparisons)
Suggest that students draw Venn diagrams to compare book characters or historic persons. Or have students compare oneself with a book character or a person from history. Have students share their comparisons to see if others agree with the responses.

Visit a Storybook Character (creative writing)

152

Have students pretend to visit a storybook or historical character for one week. Ask students to keep a day-by-day account of the activities and reactions to life as if they were the character. As a class, plan a sharing session to exchange thoughts and feelings.

Recommended Books

Blos, Joan. *A Gathering of Days: A New England Girl's Journal, 1830-32.* New York: Macmillan, 1979.

Edwards, Sally. *George Midgett's War.* New York: Macmillan, 1985.

Fleischman, Sid. *Humbug Mountain.* Boston: Little, Brown, 1982.

Fleischman, Sid. *Mr. Mysterious and Company.* Boston: Little, Brown, 1962.

Fritz, Jean. *The Cabin Faced West.* New York: Coward, 1958.

Fritz, Jean. *Homesick: My Own Story.* New York: Putnam, 1982.

George, Jean C. *Julie of the Wolves.* New York: Harper & Row, 1972.

Graeber, Charlotte T. *Grey Cloud.* New York: Macmillan, 1979.

Highwater, Jamake. *Legend Days.* New York: Harper & Row, 1984.

Hoover, H.M. *This Time of Darkness.* New York: Penguin, 1985.

Kerr, Judith. *When Hitler Stole Pink Rabbit.* New York: Putnam, 1972.

Morey, Walt. *Year of the Black Pony.* Hillsboro, OR: Blue Heron, 1989.

Mowat, Farley. *Lost in the Barrens.* New York: Little, Brown, 1962.

Sebestyen, Ouida. *Words by Heart.* Boston: Little, Brown, 1979.

Taylor, Theodore. *Walking Up a Rainbow.* New York: Dell, 1988.

Wilder, Laura Ingalls. *Little House on the Prairie.* New York: Harper & Row, 1953.

Vocabulary Review (vocabulary)

153

Help the class list 50 to 100 key words and definitions from a particular area of study. Have students make sets of cards with the words and definitions written on them. The cards can be used as individual matching games or as team games. Have teams take turns drawing word cards from a stack and matching the words with their definitions. The team with the most correct matches wins the game.

Want Ads (creative thinking)
Have students write historical want ads that might have appeared in newspapers at a particular time in history. Want ads might include:

- Wanted: Sturdy rowboat to withstand icy waters. American made, must hold men and equipment. G. Washington, Delaware Inn.
- Wanted: Persons to sew flags. Needed immediately for important government job. Betsy Ross, Philadelphia.

What Animal Would You Like to Be? (research, creative writing)
Have children choose animals they would like to be. Encourage children to share their thoughts about animals, including animal habits. Ask children to research their animals and write stories or factual essays about them. Encourage children to illustrate their writings. Or as a class, plan a mural where the children's animals meet one another.

155

Who Am I? (research, creative writing)
Ask students to imagine being a historic figure or favorite book character. Have students write autobiographies document-ing important things the characters have done. Encourage students to include personal comments unique to their characters. A personal comment might be, "I fought in a famous battle" instead of naming the battle, or "I helped make great strides for a particular group in our

156

General Douglas MacArthur

political system" instead of "I fought for women's rights."
Ask volunteers to read completed narratives aloud for
class members to identify the characters.

Recommended Books

Fritz, Jean. *And Then What Happened, Paul Revere?* New York:
Putnam, 1973.

Fritz, Jean. *The Double Life of Pocahontas.* New York: Putnam,
1983.

Fritz, Jean. *What's the Big Idea, Ben Franklin?* New York:
Putnam, 1982.

Fritz, Jean. *Where Was Patrick Henry on the 29th of May?* New
York: Putnam, 1975.

Graff, Stewart and Graff, Polly A. *Helen Keller: Toward the
Light.* Champaign, IL: Garrard, 1965.

Keller, Mollie. *Golda Meir.* New York: Watts, 1983.

Kroeber, Theodora. *Ishi, Last of His Tribe.* New York: Bantam,
1973.

McKissack, Patricia. *Martin Luther King, Jr.: A Man to
Remember.* Chicago: Childrens Press, 1984.

Morrison, Dorothy N. *Under a Strong Wind: The Adventures of
Jessie Benton Fremont.* New York: Macmillan, 1983.

Petry, Ann. *Harriet Tubman: Conductor on the Underground
Railroad.* New York: Harper & Row, 1955.

Quackenbush, Robert. *The Beagle & Mr. Flycatcher: A Story of
Charles Darwin.* Englewood Cliffs, NJ: Prentice Hall, 1983.

Quackenbush, Robert. *Quick, Annie, Give Me a Catchy Line!*
Englewood Cliffs, NJ: Prentice Hall, 1983.

Walker, Alice. *Langston Hughes, American Poet.* New York:
Harper & Row, 1974.

Yates, Elizabeth. *Amos Fortune, Free Man.* New York: E. P.
Dutton, 1967.

Who, What, Where, When (critical thinking)
Provide students with paper divided into four columns.
Head the columns with the words *who, what, where,* and
when. Choose five news items from the daily paper to

157 read aloud to the class. After reading each item, have
students fill in the columns with the correct information.
Then arrange the class into small groups. Ask the
groups to compare what they wrote on their papers.

A World's Fair (research, critical thinking)

158 With the class, plan a world's fair display of manufactured goods. Arrange the class into small groups. Have the groups choose a country and two goods that the country manufactures. As representatives of the country, ask the groups to plan a display of the manufactured goods. Have groups prepare a written account explaining the goods' importance, uses, and methods of manufacturing. Ask for a volunteer to act as chairperson to coordinate the entries from all the countries and supervise the setting up of the exhibits.

Recommended Books

Marsh, Carole. *Mystery of the World's Fair*. Bath, NC: Gallopade, 1982.
Marsh, Carole. *World's Fair Fun Trivia Book*. Bath, NC: Gallopade, 1982.
Moss, Miriam. *Fairs and Circuses*. New York: Watts, 1987.
Pierce, Jack. *The State Fair Book*. Minneapolis: Carolrhoda, 1980.

Write a Branching Story (research, creative writing, art)

159

Share with the class several nonfiction books about a civilization, country, or geographic region. Brainstorm with the children fictitious characters that might have lived at a certain time in the region. Include details, such as character descriptions, personalities, occupations, and family backgrounds. As a class, write the first chapter of a novel about the characters. Then arrange the class in groups of four or five students. Ask the groups to plan a second chapter for the novel. When the groups are finished, combine the groups' plans into a second chapter. Repeat this activity until the book is completed. Ask for volunteers to illustrate the novel. Compile the novel and illustrations into book form.

THE THEMATIC APPROACH

The thematic approach to teaching encourages the correlation of all subject areas under one topic, such as cowboys, inventions, or the Middle Ages. Its most successful methodology emphasizes student involvement in the learning process, hands-on learning activities, interaction among students in large and small working groups, as well as independent learning and culminations that provide purpose and closure for all students. This teaching method does not replace skills instruction in the subject areas. Rather, it provides a context within which the skills assume meaning for the learner.

The activities on the following pages involve skills in many subject areas. Emphasis will depend upon each teacher's objectives. The treatment of individual themes is not exhaustive, but a place to begin. Teacher and student interests will lead in many directions. Active learning experiences require careful organization to be productive.

To summarize, the thematic approach can

1. teach subject skills in a meaningful setting,
2. cut across groups and allow for equal contribution by all students,
3. provide functional use of subject skills,
4. provide activities to meet the needs of all students,
5. promote individual responsibility by providing alternatives and options in materials to be read, forms of presentation for sharing, and creative projects to be developed,
6. offer unlimited opportunities for students to read for enjoyment, as well as with a purpose in mind, and
7. widen a student's horizons by introducing a broad spectrum of literature.

Step 1: Select a Theme

This is the most important step of the procedure. The theme should be based on student interest. It may develop from a story that has been read, a TV program, a study trip, a picture, an object of particular interest, an event, or a special person. Sometimes in the interest of broadening students' knowledge, teachers must motivate interest in a particular theme. The theme should be a subject that arouses the interest of the students and has the potential for interesting research and activities.

Step 2: Prepare Your Resources

Finding books on the selected theme isn't difficult if you seek out sources. A few sources include the school librarian, the public librarian, and the school book room. Select a wide variety of books at different reading levels that are related to the theme. Collect several copies of the same book so that children can read together and discuss the material.

Ask students to contribute any books they may have on the theme. Other good sources are flea markets or garage and yard sales. Ask your school librarian to give a book talk or story hour related to the theme as an opening activity. Or prepare a book talk or story hour yourself.

Step 3: Have the Students Read Widely

Once you have introduced the theme, encourage the students to select books on the subject at their own reading level. A suggestion to read, in the interest of research, any interesting book that is at all related to the subject usually makes every one comfortable choosing books at his or her own level. Schedule ample reading times during this period so that you will be available to consult or advise.

Step 4: Encourage Students to Share Information

Encourage students to share their reading in a variety of ways, such as reading part of a book aloud, sharing what they have read, or dramatizing a scene. Such sharing might result in a panel of students who have read the same book discussing likenesses and differences in characters. Or discussion may stimulate further research on the topic. Help students formulate ideas and draw conclusions related to their reading and research.

Step 5: Offer Enjoyable Activities

Students can participate in a variety of creative activities as they present their interpretations of the material read. These activities may include dramatizations, displays, dioramas, murals, panel discussions, and interviews. It is important to set deadlines for the completion of activities to maintain student interest.

Each of the following theme sections contains activities specifically appropriate to the theme. These may be enhanced by any of the general activities (1-159).

THEMATIC ACTIVITIES

FAMILY LIFE

For young children, the family is the center of their world. Sharing information about family members and reading stories with family themes help establish connections between the familiar world and the school environment.

160 **Family Portraits** Invite children to draw family portraits. Ask the children to write sentences about each family member. Help children compile the portraits in family scrapbooks.

161 **Model Homes** Provide the class with materials to make models of their houses or apartments. Materials might include small boxes, construction paper, cardboard, paints, crayons, markers, and glue.

162 **Celebrate Grandparents' Day** Have children invite their grandparents or an older person to a Grandparents' Day party. Grandparents' Day is celebrated on the second Sunday of September. Help children plan entertainment, treats, and refreshments.

163 **Family Poetry Book** Help students collect poems about mothers, fathers, siblings, and other family members. Invite the students to choose a favorite poem to illustrate. Compile the poems and illustrations into a class booklet.

Recommended Books

Bauer, Caroline F. *My Mom Travels a Lot*. New York: Penguin, 1985.

Borack, Barbara. *Grandpa*. New York: Harper & Row, 1967.

Cole, Babette. *The Trouble with Mom*. New York: Putnam, 1986.

De Paola, Tomie. *Nana Upstairs and Nana Downstairs*. New York: Putnam, 1987.

Friedman, Ina R. *How My Parents Learned to Eat*. Boston: Houghton Mifflin, 1984.

Goffstein, M.B. *Family Scrapbook*. New York: Farrar, Straus & Giroux, 1976.

Helmering, Doris W. *I Have Two Families*. Nashville: Abingdon, 1981.

Lasker, Joe. *He's My Brother*. Niles, IL: Whitman, 1974.

Lasker, Joe. *Mothers Can Do Anything*. Niles, IL: Whitman, 1972.

Lasky, Kathryn. *I Have Four Names for My Grandfather*. Boston: Little, Brown, 1976.

Levinson, Riki. *I Go with My Family to Grandma's*. New York: E. P. Dutton, 1986.

Lewin, Hugh. *Jafta's Father*. Minneapolis: Carolrhoda, 1983.

Lewin, Hugh. *Jafta's Mother*. Minneapolis: Carolrhoda, 1983.

Lobel, Arnold. *Uncle Elephant*. New York: Harper & Row, 1986.

Locker, Thomas. *Where the River Begins*. New York: Dial, 1984.

Rylant, Cynthia. *When I Was Young in the Mountains*. New York: E. P. Dutton, 1982.

Scott, Ann H. *On Mother's Lap*. New York: McGraw-Hill, 1972.

Scott, Ann H. *Sam*. New York: McGraw-Hill, 1967.

Sonneborn, Ruth. *Friday Night Is Papa Night*. New York: Penguin, 1987.

Viorst, Judith. *I'll Fix Anthony*. New York: Harper & Row, 1969.

Williams, Barbara. *Kevin's Grandma*. New York: E. P. Dutton, 1975.

Zolotow, Charlotte. *My Grandson Lew*. New York: Harper & Row, 1974.

GETTING TO KNOW OURSELVES AND OUR CLASSMATES

Help children see themselves as important individuals. A good self-concept helps children develop good attitudes about learning and social behavior. Activities built on this theme can influence future learning.

Autobiography Ask children to bring to school some photographs of their families, pets, homes, and friends. Suggest that children place the pictures in any order on a long piece of paper. Have the children write sentences above or below the pictures. For older students, brainstorm memorable events in their lives. A few events might include the day they lost their first tooth, their first visit to an amusement park, a new baby brother or sister, or a new pet. Ask the students to choose three important events in their lives. Then have the students write paragraphs about each event in autobiographical form. Help students edit and rewrite their paragraphs. Compile the autobiographies into book form or display the writings on a bulletin board.

164

Me Mobiles With the class, brainstorm characteristics of people. A few characteristics might include freckles, black hair, blue eyes, or big smiles. Ask the students to choose three or four unique characteristics of themselves. Supply the class with paper, markers, string, and coat hangers to create their own "Me Mobiles." Hang the mobiles from wire stretched across the room.

165

Name Acrostics Explain to the class what an acrostic is. Use someone's name as an example. A name acrostic for James might be Jolly Ambitious Mild-Mannered Energetic Sociable. Have the students write their names vertically on a sheet of paper. Ask students to write one or two words about themselves for each letter. Make a bulletin-board display of the name acrostics.

166

Names Are Special Share the stories of *Rumpelstiltskin* or *Tikki Tikki Tembo* with the class.

167

Explain that in traditional fairy tales, names are often concealed because the one who knows a person's name has power over that person. Ask students to write their full names on a sheet of paper. Brainstorm a list of questions that someone might ask about a person's name. These might include: How did you get your first and middle names? Who decided to name you that? Do you like your names? If you could change names, what would your choices be? Do you have a nickname? How did you get the nickname? Who calls you by your nickname? Divide the class into groups of two. Have the groups ask questions about their names. Allow ten minutes, signalling after five minutes for the second child's turn to begin. Encourage children to talk with their parents about their names. The next day, have the children write name stories using the information they have gathered. Bind the stories into a class book.

Recommended Books

Bayer, Jane. *A, My Name Is Alice.* New York: Dial, 1984.
Davis, Gibbs. *The Other Emily.* Boston: Houghton Mifflin, 1984.
Meltzer, Milton. *A Book About Names.* New York: Harper & Row, 1984.
Mosel, Arlene. *Tikki Tikki Tembo.* New York: Holt, 1968.
Waber, Bernard. *But Names Will Never Hurt Me.* Boston: Houghton Mifflin, 1976.

168 **Me Bags** Provide the class with paper bags and materials for decorating. Have students draw pictures of themselves on the outside of the bags and use yarn, ribbon, cloth, and other items to decorate the bags. For the inside of the bag, have the children draw or write something special about themselves on a piece of paper. Have students share their "Me Bags" with each other. Older children might write three statements about themselves on the back of the bag for others to read.

169 **A Book About Me** Explain to students that they are going to make a book about themselves. Write on the chalkboard or duplicate the following suggestions for the students. Discuss the ideas with the class. Then provide paper folded in book form for the students' books. Encourage students to share their books with each other.

- Imagine a special place of your very own. On one page of your book, describe this place, tell where it is, what you do there, and why you like to be in your special place. Draw a picture.
- At the top of one page, draw a big star. Wish on your star and write three wishes that you hope will come true.
- On another page, make a list of your five favorite stories. Draw the character you like best.
- Make a picture of yourself wearing your favorite outfit on the next page. Below, describe the outfit, tell where you are going, and why it is your favorite outfit.
- Think about a special day you would like to have. Write about that special day on another page.
- What age would you most like to be? Think of all your reasons and write them on the next page of your book.
- Make at least three more pages using your own ideas for your special book.
- Illustrate the cover of your book. Be sure to include the title and author.

Person of the Week Select a week of the school year for each child in your class to be "The Person of the Week." Share the activity with the children's parents. Designate bulletin-board space for "The Person of the Week." On Monday, with the class, write a paragraph about the special person and post the paragraph on the bulletin board. Encourage the child to bring special items and photographs from home for display. Invite the children's family to school during the special week. Encourage older students to write and illustrate stories about the selected person. Bind the stories in a book for the child to keep.

170

Recommended Books

De Regniers, Beatrice S. *Everyone Is Good for Something.* Boston: Houghton Mifflin, 1980.

Moncure, Jane B. *The Look Book.* Chicago: Childrens Press, 1982.

Moncure, Jane B. *The Touch Book.* Chicago: Childrens Press, 1982.

Moncure, Jane B. *What Your Nose Knows!* Chicago: Childrens Press, 1982.

Sharmat, Marjorie W. *I'm Terrific.* New York: Holiday, 1977.

LEARNING ABOUT OUR SCHOOL

These activities give children the opportunity to explore and use newly acquired skills in a familiar, friendly environment—school.

171

Exploring the School Environment With the class, take a walking tour of the school and playground. Return to the classroom and list the areas visited. Help the class sketch a floor plan of the school on the chalkboard. Discuss the room sizes, length of halls, and other factors. Provide students with sheets of paper to make their own floor plan of the school. Display the floor plans on a bulletin board.

172

Getting to Know Our School Help the class make a directory of school helpers. Have students write invitations to the helpers asking them to visit the classroom for interviews. Prior to their visits, discuss interviewing and develop a simple format with the class. During the interviews, have students take notes of the responses or tape record the interview. If students are older, they may interview individuals in their offices. Then have the older students bring the interviewee to the classroom. Suggest that students introduce the person to the rest of the class using information from their notes. Suggest that students write articles about the helpers. Information, with illustrations, may be organized and bound into a school directory. Ask students to write and deliver thank-you notes to the personnel along with copies of the directory.

173

Classroom Yellow Pages Examine the yellow pages of the telephone directory with the class. Discuss the arrangement of entries by subject headings and the reasoning for this format. Help students look for items of interest. Note some of the services listed. Have the students make a similar yellow pages phone directory for the classroom. Ask students to make a list of jobs or services that they do especially well. Jobs and services might include school subjects they can tutor, sports in which they excel, and musical instruments that the students play. Encourage students to make other suggestions.

174

Learning Our School's Story Discuss the history of the school with the class. A few questions that might be asked are: How many children have siblings who attended the school or are attending the school now? Did anyone's parents attend? Did any famous people attend the school? When was the school built? Is the school part of a consolidated school district? Make a chart of what the class knows and wants to know about the school. Brainstorm with the students where information might be found. Encourage students to investigate some of these ideas. Ask the superintendent and principal to visit the classroom and share information about the school. Help students complete the chart as information is found. Ask for a few volunteers to write a report using the information gathered.

Recommended Books

Allard, Harry and Marshall, James. *Miss Nelson Is Missing.* Boston: Houghton Mifflin, 1977.

Arnold, Caroline. *Where Do You Go to School?* New York: Watts, 1982.

Breinberg, Petronella. *Shawn Goes to School.* New York: Harper & Row, 1974.

Christian, Mary B. *Swamp Monsters.* New York: Dial, 1983.

Cohen, Miriam. *First Grade Takes a Test.* New York: Greenwillow Books, 1980.

Feder, Paula K. *Where Does the Teacher Live?* New York: E. P. Dutton, 1979.

Giff, Patricia R. *The Beast in Ms. Rooney's Room.* New York: Dell, 1984.

Howe, James. *The Day the Teacher Went Bananas.* New York:

E. P. Dutton, 1984.

Loeper, John J. *Going to School in 1776.* New York: Macmillan, 1973.

Loeper, John J. *Going to School in 1876.* New York: Macmillan, 1984.

Noble, Trinka H. *The Day Jimmy's Boa Ate the Wash.* New York: Dial, 1980.

Oppenheim, Joanne. *Mrs. Peloki's Class Play.* New York: Putnam, 1983.

Yashima, Taro. *Crow Boy.* New York: Penguin, 1955.

EXPLORING THE NEIGHBORHOOD AND COMMUNITY

Children acquire understanding of basic human needs and society's means of meeting them by exploring areas outside of the classroom. Concepts developed first by studying the local neighborhood and community are the basis for later focus on societies worldwide.

175

Mapping the School Neighborhood With the class, take a walking tour of the school neighborhood. Ask the children to notice the buildings, houses, and people that they see. After the walk, make a chart of what was seen. Use categories, such as buildings, vehicles, and people. Provide a large outline map of the school neighborhood. (A map is usually available from the superintendent or the transportation director.) Have children draw and cut out pictures of their homes. Place the homes on the map. Use the information from the chart and have children make pictures of the other buildings found in the neighborhood. Attach these pictures to the map. Encourage children to make other objects to place on the map. Other objects might include cars, trucks, people, and parks. Display the completed map on a classroom wall. Have children practice composing sentences giving exact locations of their homes and how to walk from their homes to other places on the map.

176 **It's in the Bag** Give the children paper bags. Take a neighborhood walk and ask the children to place ten items in their bags. After the walk, have the children share their items with the class. Provide children with paper, glue, and crayons to create a collage using their found items. Display the collages on a bulletin board titled "Neighborhood Collages."

177 **Make a Model of the Community** Discuss how neighborhoods are part of a community. List important features of the community on the chalkboard. On the floor or on a large table, help the class plan and lay out their community. Use boxes, tagboard, and other material to construct the model. Display the completed model in a central location of the school.

178 **A Directory for the Neighborhood or Community** Help the class list all the work places in the neighborhood or community on the chalkboard or on a chart. Arrange the class into small groups. Ask the groups to research the occupations that exist in the community. Have the groups write short descriptions of the occupations, including the training that is needed to work at that occupation. Help the class compile the information in booklet form.

179 **Occupations Fair** Invite five or six community workers to visit the classroom for an Occupations Fair. Ask workers to explain their jobs in the community. Set up stations for the community workers and rotate students through the stations. Or have large group presentations for the entire class.

180 **Future Careers** Read aloud several books dealing with careers. Have the students draw pictures and write stories about what they would like to do. Suggest that the students dress like their chosen career and present their stories to the class. Bind the stories in book form for the class library.

Class Grocery Store With the class, visit a grocery store or supermarket. Ask children to notice the different sections of the store and the merchandise sold in each section. After returning to the classroom, discuss the sections needed for a classroom grocery store. Ask **181** children to bring empty grocery containers from home. Have the children use grocery store ads to determine the prices of the grocery items in the classroom grocery. As a class, choose a name for the store. Encourage children to write display ads and radio spots for the store. Use the store to practice smart shopping and making change.

A Variety or Department Store Visit a variety or department store in the community or request that parents take children to a variety or department store. Help children identify the employees, the various depart- **182** ments, and the items sold in the store. Using butcher paper and cardboard boxes, have groups of students make roller movies about a variety or department store. Suggest that different groups show various departments in the store.

Food for the Community Make a bulletin board captioned "Where in the World Does Our Breakfast Come From?" Place the name where each food comes from on one side and the name of food items or pictures on the other. Food items might include bananas, or- **183** anges, cereal, sugar, milk, bread, and eggs. Connect foods to the appropriate place with colored string. Under each object, place blank paper for notes. When the bulletin board is complete, help the class write a group article about the origin of their breakfasts.

Goods Come to Our Community Encourage students to speculate where their blue jeans or tennis shoes were made and how they arrived at the stores. Have students interview local store owners for answers to their ques- **184** tions, as well as consulting reference materials. Display worn tennis shoes or pairs of jeans. Brainstorm words and phrases to describe the shoes or jeans. Have stu- dents write stories entitled "A Day in the Life of My Tennis Shoes," or "The Hard Life of a Pair of Jeans."

185

Building Materials Assemble a collection of building materials, such as bricks, 2 x 4's, finished boards, and nails. Discuss the types of building materials used in the local community. Help students identify reasons for the use of particular materials in their community. Have students draw pictures of the different styles of buildings in their neighborhood and community. Ask students to construct a model building using plaster, cardboard, Lincoln logs, or Lego bricks. Have students write captions for their buildings and have a class display. Suggest that students research early buildings in their community. Encourage the researchers to create a display of former buildings. The local historical society or public library may have books available for students' use.

186

ABC Community Collect a variety of alphabet books for students to examine. Brainstorm with the class how a community ABC book might be made. Have children illustrate the letters of the alphabet with items found in the community. When the pages are completed, compile the pages into book form. As an extension, have the class make several ABC community books and present the books to the school librarian or to a lower-grade class.

Recommended Books

Aitken, Amy. *Ruby, The Red Knight*. New York: Bradbury, 1983.

Arnold, Caroline. *What Is a Community?* New York: Watts, 1982.

Bundt, Nancy. *Fire Station Book*. Minneapolis: Carolrhoda, 1981.

Florian, Douglas. *People Working*. New York: Harper & Row, 1983.

Gibbons, Gail. *Department Store*. New York: Harper & Row, 1984.

Gibbons, Gail. *Fire! Fire!* New York: Harper & Row, 1984.

Gibbons, Gail. *The Post Office Book*. New York: Harper & Row, 1982.

Horwitz, Joshua. *Night Markets: Bringing Food to the City*. New York: Harper & Row, 1986.

Howe, James. *The Hospital Book*. Southbridge, MA: Crown, 1981.

Pierce, Jack. *The Freight Train Book*. Minneapolis: Carolrhoda, 1981.

Rey, H. A. and Rey, Margret. *Curious George Goes to the Hospital.* Boston: Houghton Mifflin, 1973.

Rockwell, Anne and Rockwell, Harlow. *The Supermarket.* New York: Macmillan, 1979.

Smith, Betsy. *A Day in the Life of a Firefighter.* Mahwah, NJ: Troll, 1981.

Ventura, Piero. *Piero Ventura's Book of Cities.* New York: Random House, 1975.

Zion, Gene. *Dear Garbage Man.* New York: Harper & Row, 1988.

Zolotow, Charlotte. *Someday.* New York: Harper & Row, 1965.

AUTUMN

Seasonal observations are especially important to young children. The observations help establish a sense of time and an understanding of the relationships between events and the passing year. In the school calendar, autumn is a time of beginning. Seasonal activities help children develop skills and maintain growth. The autumn theme is an example of seasonal activities. Similar planning may be done for winter, spring, and summer.

187

Autumn Leaves Go on a leaf collection walk with the class. Help the children press the leaves between pages of heavy books using waxed paper to protect the pages. Then have children arrange the leaves on construction paper and glue in place. Cover with contact paper or press between sheets of waxed paper and iron. Or mount the leaves on a bulletin board with poems about autumn. Encourage children to write their own poems about autumn to display with the leaves as well.

188 **Celebrate the Autumn Harvest** Cut a large cornucopia out of brown construction paper and place it on the bulletin board. On the chalkboard, help the class list as many autumn fruits and vegetables as possible. Provide the class with pictures of real fruits and vegetables as guides. Then have students make fruits and vegetables from colored paper to fill the cornucopia. Encourage the children to tear the construction paper rather than cutting out shapes.

189 **Recipes for Harvest Fruits and Vegetables** Discuss favorite recipes for fruits and vegetables. Provide cookbooks for the class to research recipes. Ask the children to find favorite recipes to copy and illustrate with black pen or pencil. Duplicate and bind the recipes in book form for the class.

190 **Harvest Vegetables Tasting Party** Have a vegetable tasting party with the class. Ask students to bring raw or cooked vegetables to school to share. Discuss various recipes that can be prepared with the vegetables. Encourage students to research the origin of the vegetables. Ask the students to share their information with the class.

191 **Autumn Fruit and Vegetable Poetry** Help students find poems about fruits and vegetables. Ask the students to choose a favorite poem to practice reciting. Have the students present their poems to the rest of the class. Or use the poems for choral reading.

192 **Pumpkin Descriptions** Bring several pumpkins to class. Have students feel the skin of the pumpkins, smell the pumpkins, and describe the pumpkins' color and shape. Cut the pumpkins open. Discuss the color and texture of the insides. On the chalkboard, help the class list words and phrases that describe the pumpkins. Encourage students, individually or in pairs, to write descriptions of the pumpkins. Or write a group poem, helping students use the list of descriptive words and phrases. If the pumpkins are cooking pumpkins, help the children make pumpkin pies.

Recommended Books

Allington, Richard L. *Autumn.* Milwaukee: Raintree, 1985.

Hopkins, Lee Bennett, ed. *Merrily Comes Our Harvest In: Poems for Thanksgiving.* San Diego: Harcourt Brace Jovanovich, 1978.

Perl, Lila. *Hunter's Stew and Hangtown Fry: What Pioneer America Ate and Why.* Boston: Houghton Mifflin, 1979.

Perl, Lila. *Slumps, Grunts, and Snickerdoodles: What Colonial America Ate and Why.* Merlin, OR: Clarion, 1979.

Tresselt, Alvin. *Autumn Harvest.* New York: Lothrop, 1951.

Zolotow, Charlotte. *Say It!* New York: Greenwillow Books, 1980.

FRUITS AND VEGETABLES

The harvest theme leads naturally into activities involving foods. Two popular food celebrations are Apple Day and Potato Day. Plan a day or a week's worth of activities around one fruit or vegetable. Using a fruit or vegetable that has several varieties works well.

193 **Fruit and Vegetable Math** Purchase an assortment or bag of one type of fruit or vegetable. Have the class count the fruits or vegetables. Have children arrange the produce in sets. Try weighing and cutting the produce in different sections. Discuss the meaning of halves, fourths, and eighths.

194 **Fruit and Vegetable Election** If a variety of one type of produce is available, such as Navel, Valencia, or Sunkist oranges, for example, have the class taste the different varieties. Have the children vote for their favorite variety using ballots. Ask for volunteers to count the ballots. Make a bar graph of the election results.

195 **Fruit and Vegetable Science** Cut produce so that students may see the seeds or the insides. Help children research how produce grows. If possible, have children plant seeds of several fruits or vegetables. Chart the growth of the seeds.

196 **Fruit and Vegetable Art** Help the class make prints using sections of fruits or vegetables. Display the prints on a bulletin board. Or make placemats by covering the prints with contact paper or wax paper.

197 **Cooking Fruits and Vegetables** Have the class find recipes that use different fruits and vegetables. Help children prepare several of the recipes. Have a sample tasting party.

198 **Fruit and Vegetable Vocabulary** Make a class list of fruit and vegetable words. Have the class make shape books of the fruits or vegetables. Using the vocabulary, have the children write stories, poems, and riddles in their books.

199 **Fruit and Vegetable Regions** Prepare an outline map of the world or country. Have the children research regions where fruits and vegetables are grown. Mark the regions on the outline map. Ask a few volunteers to determine the growing seasons of some of the fruits and vegetables. Compare the different growing seasons in the different regions.

200 **Fruit and Vegetable Feeling Bag** Place a fruit or vegetable in a paper bag. Have the children feel the fruit or vegetable and guess what it is. Try this with several varieties. Discuss how the fruit or vegetable is eaten. Ask the children to taste the raw fruit or vegetable. Discuss the taste and texture.

201 **Find the Fruit or Vegetable** Provide each child with the same fruit or vegetable to study. Ask children to examine their fruit or vegetable carefully, noticing any spots or unusual marks. Place a piece of tape on the children's fruit or vegetable. Have the children write their names on the tape. Then place the fruits or vegetables on a table so that the names don't show. Ask the children to pick out their own fruit or vegetable. Encourage the children to explain how they identified their own fruits or vegetables.

Marketing Fruits and Vegetables As a class, re-search one specific fruit or vegetable. Arrange the class into groups. Ask each group to research a specific topic about the fruit or vegetable. A few topics might include where the fruit or vegetable originated, where the product is grown, how it is grown, how it is harvested, shipped, and marketed. Compile the research into a class booklet.

202

Fruit or Vegetable Games Arrange the class into four or five groups. Have a relay race carrying a fruit or vegetable on a spoon or flat pan. Play Hot Fruit or Vegetable like the game Hot Potato. Play a version of Duck, Duck, Goose, where fruit and vegetable names are used.

203

Recommended Books

Aliki. *Story of Johnny Appleseed.* Englewood Cliffs, NJ: Prentice Hall, 1987.

Blocksma, Mary. *Apple Tree! Apple Tree!* Chicago: Childrens Press, 1983.

Devlin, Wende and Devlin, Harry. *Cranberry Thanksgiving.* New York: Putnam, 1971.

Gemming, Elizabeth. *Cranberry Book.* New York: Putnam, 1983.

Haddad, Helen R. *Potato Printing.* New York: Harper & Row, 1981.

Johnson, Sylvia A. *Apple Trees.* Minneapolis: Carolrhoda, 1983.

Scheer, Julian. *Rain Makes Applesauce.* New York: Holiday, 1964.

Selsam, Millicent. *More Potatoes.* New York: Harper & Row, 1972.

Sobol, Harriet A. *A Book of Vegetables.* New York: Putnam, 1984.

Turner, Dorothy. *Potatoes.* Minneapolis: Carolrhoda 1989.

BREADS OF THE WORLD

A study based on breads of the world can be the basis of a wide variety of enriching activities. The activities will provide children the opportunity to share their cultural backgrounds. Historically, bread dates back 10,000 years. Over the centuries, bread has been made from a wide variety of ingredients, including acorns and manioc roots.

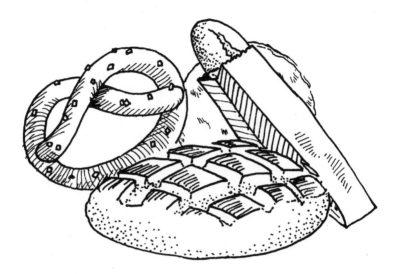

204   **Bread Research** With the class, make a list of different kinds of bread and their origins. Encourage students to use some of the following resources: home, bakeries, grocery stores, and reference books. A list might include knackebrod from Sweden, scones from Scotland, stollen and bagels from Germany, croissants from France, corn pone from southern United States, chapatti from India, tortillas from Mexico, and brioche from France.

205   **A Bread Map** Make a world map and place an illustration of each bread mentioned in the previous activity in its appropriate place. Read stories and sing songs from each of the countries. Encourage students to research the appropriate culture and the countries. Older students may wish to research the origins of cultivated grains used in the various breads. If possible, sample some of the breads.

206   **Bread Baking** Visit a bakery to watch bread being made. Then plan to bake some bread with the class. Write a recipe on large chart paper. Have children work in small groups with adult supervision to prepare the bread. Help children divide the duties of mixing the bread so that all have a chance to help.

Recommended Books

Hautzig, Esther. *Holiday Treats.* New York: Macmillan, 1983.

Walker, Barbara. *Little House Cookbook: Frontier Foods from Laura Ingalls Wilder's Classic Stories.* New York: Harper & Row, 1979.

HOLIDAYS

Holidays offer the opportunity for cultural experiences. Children should be encouraged to share family traditions with the class.

207 **Halloween Reading** Arrange with the school librarian to bring your class to the library for a special reading of Halloween-related books. After the class has read or listened to several Halloween books, ask children to think of some Halloween vocabulary. Make a list of the words on the chalkboard. Group the words into categories and write the words on a chart. Have students use the words to write stories, poems, or skits. An additional activity using the vocabulary might be to alphabetize the words in the various categories. Arrange the class into small groups and have each group alphabetize one category.

208 **Halloween Animal Study** Help children list Halloween animal names on the chalkboard. Arrange the class into small groups. Have the groups write the animal names on sheets of construction paper. Display the names on a bulletin board. As the children read Halloween stories, have them write related words on the animal papers. Use the various animals and related words to write class or individual stories, reports, riddles, and skits.

209 **Scary Halloween Tree** Place a bare branch in a pot in the classroom. Have children draw and hang illustrations of scary Halloween words on the branches. Then sit under the tree to read aloud Halloween stories.

210 **Halloween Obstacle Race** Create an obstacle course in the gym or in a large classroom. Children try to reach the pumpkin patch in the center of the room, passing through several obstacles. Appoint one of the children to be the "Spooky Scarecrow." The Spooky Scarecrow wanders about looking for trespassers in his pumpkin patch. Anyone the Scarecrow tags must go back to the beginning. Children are "safe" from the Scarecrow if they squat and put both hands on the floor. Upon reaching the pumpkin patch, children collect a small prize from the Great Pumpkin, but must exit hurriedly before the Scarecrow catches them.

211 **Halloween Witches' Brew** Purchase or ask students to bring the food items listed below to school. Mix together the food items. Compose a chant with the students to recite as each ingredient is added. Then share a cup of witches' brew with the class. This might be used as a Halloween party activity. Read favorite Halloween stories while eating the witches' brew.

> 1 cup blood drops (red-hots)
> 1 cup owl eyes (hazel nuts)
> 1 cup cat eyes (blanched almonds)
> 1 cup chicken toenails (candy corn)
> 1 cup colored flies (chocolate-covered candies)
> 1 cup butterfly wings (corn chips)
> 1 cup ants (raisins)
> 1 cup earthworms (cheese puffs)
> 1 cup cobwebs (crackers broken in half)
> 1 cup snake eyes (salted peanuts)
> 1 cup lizard gizzard (dried fruit)
> 1 cup bat bones (shoestring potatoes)
> 1 cup cat claws (shelled sunflower seeds)

Halloween Pumpkin Day Display a pumpkin, real or paper, prominently in the classroom with a sign stating, "Today is Pumpkin Day." Examples of activities include:

- Hold a contest for the longest list of words made from the letters in the words PUMPKIN or JACK-O'-LANTERN.
- Write pumpkin-related questions on strips of paper on a bulletin board. Have students place their answers in a pumpkin-decorated box. Near the end of the day ask for volunteers to check the answers. Give pumpkin treats to those with the correct responses. Questions might include: Is a pumpkin a fruit or a vegetable? When did carving jack-o'-lanterns become a custom? How do pumpkins grow? How many varieties of pumpkins are there? Where are pumpkins grown?

212

Halloween Pumpkin Pantomime Print the following directions on small pumpkin cutouts. Have children draw from a pumpkin container and perform the pantomimes.

- Pretend you are a black cat walking on fence posts on Halloween night.
- Pretend you are a witch stirring a brew. Drop in several objects and cackle their description.
- Pretend you are walking down a dark street on Halloween night.
- Pretend you have seen a ghost staring in the window.
- Pretend you are walking into a haunted house as the clock strikes twelve.
- Pretend you are an owl hooting at midnight.

213

Recommended Books

Asch, Frank. *Popcorn*. New York: Parents Magazine, 1979.

Bradbury, Ray. *The Halloween Tree*. New York: Knopf, 1988.

Coville, Bruce. *The Monster's Ring*. New York: Pantheon, 1982.

Hamilton, Virginia. *Willie Bea and the Time the Martians Landed*. New York: Greenwillow Books, 1983.

Hoban, Lillian. *Arthur's Halloween Costume*. New York: Harper & Row, 1984.

Johnston, Tony. *Vanishing Pumpkin*. New York: Putnam, 1984.

Kellogg, Steven. *The Mystery of the Flying Orange Pumpkin*. New

York: Dial, 1980.

Marshall, Edward. *Space Case.* New York: Dial, 1980.

Prelutsky, Jack. *It's Halloween.* New York: Greenwillow Books, 1977.

Stevenson, James. *That Terrible Halloween Night.* New York: Greenwillow Books, 1980.

Zolotow, Charlotte. *A Tiger Called Thomas.* New York: Lothrop, 1988.

214 **Veterans Day** Bring to class poppies distributed by Veterans of Foreign Wars. Discuss the purpose of selling poppies. Or invite a committee member of the Veterans of Foreign Wars to come speak to the class about the purpose of selling poppies. If possible, have children make their own poppies to wear. Discuss what war is, why wars are fought, and what happens to people and places in time of war. Help children speculate how wars can be stopped or prevented.

Recommended Books

Fitzhugh, Louise and Scoppettone, Sandra. *Bang Bang You're Dead.* New York: Harper & Row, 1986.

Lobel, Anita. *Potatoes, Potatoes.* New York: Harper & Row, 1984.

215 **The Thanksgiving Story** Share with the class fiction and nonfiction material about the founding of the Plymouth colony and the events that led to the first Thanksgiving. Have the class act out the story using one of the following suggestions.

- Arrival at Plymouth Rock: sighting land, disembarking, building a shelter.
- Passing the winter: cutting wood, indoor activities, meeting Indians, going to church.
- First spring: clearing land, preparing soil, planting, getting help from the Indians.
- First Thanksgiving: harvesting the crops, preparing the feast, arrival of Indians, prayer of thanks, games and races, Indian departure.

216 **Thanksgiving Turkey Talk** Introduce the topic of turkeys by visiting a local turkey farm or viewing films and books about turkeys. If possible, display a variety of turkey feathers for children to examine. Ask students to observe the turkeys carefully, whether in books, films, or live turkeys. Group the class into pairs. Explain that each child is to describe a turkey for the other child when you give the signal. Then after one minute, signal for the other partner to begin describing a turkey. Repeat this activity three or four times. Then ask students to draw and write brief descriptions of turkeys. Display the drawings and descriptions on a bulletin board.

217 **Thanksgiving Turkey Research** Help students make a list of what they know about turkeys and a second list of what they would like to learn. Write the second list in the form of questions on turkey-shaped paper. Have students research the questions in reference books. As answers are found, have the children write the answers on the turkey shapes. Display the turkey-shape questions and answers on a bulletin board. Write a group report about turkeys, combining the information from all the turkey shapes.

218 **Thanksgiving Turkey Math** Bring to class grocery ads that show the cost of turkeys. Help students determine the price of turkeys weighing different amounts. If possible, contact a hatchery or turkey farm and ask about the cost of raising turkeys. Share the information with the class.

Recommended Books

Anderson, Joan. *The First Thanksgiving Feast.* Merlin, OR: Clarion, 1984.

Behrens, June. *Feast of Thanksgiving.* Chicago: Childrens Press, 1974.

Dalgliesh, Alice. *The Thanksgiving Story.* New York: Scribners, 1954.

DeLage, Ida. *Pilgrim Children Come to Plymouth.* Champaign, IL: Garrard, 1981.

Hopkins, Lee B., ed. *Merrily Comes Our Harvest In: Poems for Thanksgiving.* San Diego: Harcourt Brace Jovanovich, 1978.

Kessel, Joyce K. *Squanto and the First Thanksgiving.* Minneapolis: Carolrhoda, 1983.

Lavine, Sigmund and Scuro, Vincent. *The Wonders of Turkeys.* New York: Putnam, 1984.

Schatell, Brian. *Farmer Goff and His Turkey, Sam.* New York: Harper & Row, 1982.

Sewall, Marcia. *The Pilgrims of Plimoth.* New York: Macmillan, 1986.

219 **Christmas Wreaths** Help the children cut ring shapes 12 to 15 inches in diameter by 3 inches wide. Provide the class with food items, such as nuts in their shells, various shapes of pasta, beans, peas, popcorn kernels, and wrapped hard candy. Have the children glue the food items on the wreath cutouts. Use large red or green bows made from crepe paper to decorate the wreaths. Or children might make wreaths for winter birds. Have the class investigate appropriate foods for the birds.

220 **Christmas Trees** Have children research how and where Christmas trees are grown. On a map of North America, have the class locate Christmas tree regions. Visit a Christmas tree farm or a lot where trees are sold. Have children ask about the different types of trees available. If possible, obtain a small branch from each type of tree to display in the classroom. Help students list the types of Christmas trees. If possible, obtain several seedlings and raise trees as a class. Have students research some of the following questions: How are trees brought to the community? What contribution does the Christmas tree industry make to the national and local economies? What purposes does tree farming serve in management of natural resources?

221 **Celebrate the New Year** Introduce the New Year by reading books or stories on the subject. Locate any cities or countries mentioned in the readings. Discuss customs of the various countries concerning the New Year. One example might be in China where the people celebrate the Chinese New Year. Explain to the class the Chinese lunar calendar. Help children find the animals representing the year of their births. Help the children construct a paper dragon. Parade the dragon around the school.

Recommended Books

Behrens, June. *Gung Hay Fat Choy*. Chicago: Childrens Press, 1982.
Cheng, Hou-Tien. *Chinese New Year*. New York: Holt, 1976.
Kelley, Emily. *Happy New Year*. Minneapolis: Lerner, 1984.

222 **Valentine's Day Post Office** Collect books and materials on the post office for the class to read. Ask the clerk at the post office for teaching materials available from the U.S. Postal Service. Provide each child with an address according to the classroom seating chart. Help the class make mailboxes from shoeboxes or other types of boxes. Create a large main mailbox for all incoming mail. Incoming mail might include daily papers, notes from other students, or notes about school activities. Appoint postmasters to distribute mail daily from the main mailbox to the individual boxes. Use the post office setup for the distribution of the children's valentines, too.

Recommended Books

Gibbons, Gail. *The Post Office Book.* New York: Crowell, 1982.
Roth, Harold. *First Class! The Postal System in Action.* New York: Pantheon, 1983.

223 **Valentine's Day Hearts** Ask the school nurse to show students how to count their pulse and heartbeats. Help children research how the heart works and how to keep it well and strong. Call your local heart association and ask for any appropriate educational materials available.

224 **A St. Patrick's Day Visit** On St. Patrick's Day, leave traces around the classroom of a leprechaun's visit. A few examples include green balloons, green candy, green bookmarks, or green pencils. Make a trail of footprints left by the leprechaun, using green footprints cut from construction paper taped to the floor. Meet the children outside the classroom door and explain that you think a leprechaun has visited the room. Pretend to catch one in a paper bag in which you have previously put a small hole and a note saying, "Got away! See you next St. Patrick's Day." Fasten the bag with a rubber band and put it on your desk. Later in the day, open the bag and discover the hole and the note. Read the note to the class. Discuss how the leprechaun might have entered and left the room. Ask the students to do one of the following activities:

• Write a story from the leprechaun's point of view— how he or she came into the room, what the leprechaun saw and found, what it was like spending a day in the bag, and what the leprechaun heard.
• Draw a picture of where you think the leprechaun is now. Write a description about the picture.

• Write the story of the leprechaun's visit as if you were a newspaper reporter.

Recommended Book

Balian, Lorna. *Leprechauns Never Lie*. Nashville: Abingdon, 1980.

225 **Passover Seder** Celebrate Passover, a Jewish festival commemorating the Israelites' flight from Egypt and slavery. Prepare a seder, the traditional meal, using a *Haggadah*, a small book telling the story of Passover. Or perform only the symbolic part of the service. You may obtain a Haggadah from some bookstores, or contact a synagogue in your area.

226 **Groundhog's Day Shadows** Arrange the class into groups of two. Help the students do the following experiment outside. Standing in the sun in the early morning, have the pairs of children trace each other's shadows on butcher paper or newsprint. Record the time of day. Repeat the shadow tracing at noon and just before the school day ends. Ask the children to cut out the three shadows and compare them. Help students draw conclusions about the movement of the sun and the size of their shadows. An alternate experiment might be to try the following activity. Take the class outside and ask these questions: How tall can you make your shadow? How short? Make your shadow stand on one leg. Make your shadow's arms disappear. Can you put your foot on your shadow's head? Join three other people and make the biggest shadow you can make. Finish the activity with a game of shadow tag.

Recommended Books

Cauley, Lorinda B. *The New House*. San Diego: Harcourt Brace Jovanovich, 1981.
Cendrars, Blaise. *Shadow*. New York: Scribners, 1982.
De Regniers, Beatrice S. and Gordon, Isabel. *The Shadow Book*. San Diego: Harcourt Brace Jovanovich, 1960.
Goor, Ron and Goor, Nancy. *Shadows: Here, There, and Everywhere*. New York: Crowell, 1981.
Simon, Seymour. *Shadow Magic*. New York: Lothrop, 1985.
Tompert, Ann. *Nothing Sticks Like a Shadow*. Boston: Houghton Mifflin, 1984.

227

Easter Bonnets Share books and pictures of Easter bonnets with the class. Discuss the various decorations on the hats. Provide the class with materials to make hats of their own. Materials might include construction paper, yarn scraps, feathers, and ribbon. Use paper sacks as the base for the children's hats. When the hats are complete, have an Easter bonnet parade.

Recommended Books

Keats, Ezra Jack. *Jenny's Hat.* New York: Harper & Row, 1966.
Slobodkina, Esphyr. *Caps for Sale.* New York: Harper & Row, 1987.

228

Mother's Day Plant Sale In March, arrange with a local nursery for the purchase of several flats of small flowering plants. Help the class set up a company to sell the plants. Discuss what might be done with any profit made. Help students borrow funds (from the school office) to purchase plants. Help the class negotiate a note for the loan and assign responsibility of caring for the plants. Close to Mother's Day, have children save and cut milk cartons for transplanting the individual plants. Have students make posters advertising their plant sale. Appoint a group of students to visit each classroom announcing the event. Hold the plant sale and pay off the note. Discuss the amount of the profit and help the class decide what to do with the proceeds.

PETS

Children's fascination with animals makes this topic an easy one to introduce and develop. The theme lends itself to research, diaries, descriptive writing, and the learning of science concepts.

229 **Unusual Pets** Ask children to name animals, wild and domestic, that would make unusual pets. Have the class use wildlife books, *Ranger Rick* magazines, and other resources to develop an extensive list. Encourage children to write stories about an unusual animal they would like to have as a pet.

230 **Pet Reports** Help the class list general questions that should be answered before choosing a pet. Arrange students in groups of four or five. Ask the children to choose animals to research. Allow time for students to study their animals, taking simple notes to use in reporting to their group. Have students share information in their small groups. Encourage the children to ask each other questions. Mix the groups and have them share again. Ask the students to write "How I Would Care for My Pet" using the information they have gathered. Articles might be mounted as posters or bound in a book.

231 **Pet Arguments** Discuss unusual pets people might have. Ask students to think of arguments persuading their parents to allow them to have an unusual pet. Help children argue persuasively by offering reasons for not keeping unusual pets. After oral discussion, have students write their arguments. Ask students to exchange papers. Then have the students reply to the arguments as a parent might.

Recommended Books

Arnold, Caroline. *Pets Without Homes.* Merlin, OR: Clarion, 1983.

Burningham, John. *The Rabbit.* New York: Crowell, 1975.

Chrystie, Frances. *Pets.* Boston: Little, Brown, 1974.

DeJong, Meindert. *Shadrach.* New York: Harper & Row, 1953.

Dunn, Phoebe and Dunn, Judy. *Animals of Buttercup Farm.* New York: Random House, 1981.

Gackenbach, Dick. *Do You Love Me?* Merlin, OR: Clarion, 1979.

Goodall, Jane. *The Chimpanzee Family Book.* Saxonville, MA: Picture, 1989.

Haywood, Carolyn. *Eddie's Menagerie.* Mahwah, NJ: Troll, 1987.

Hess, Lilo. *Diary of a Rabbit.* New York: Scribners, 1982.

Hess, Lilo. *Making Friends with Guinea Pigs.* New York: Scribners, 1983.

Keats, Ezra Jack. *Pet Show!* New York: Macmillan, 1987.

Kellogg, Steven. *Can I Keep Him?* New York: Dial, 1971.

Lavies, Bianca. *It's an Armadillo!* New York: E. P. Dutton, 1989.

North, Sterling. *Rascal: A Memoir of a Better Era.* New York: E. P. Dutton, 1984.

Parish, Peggy. *No More Monsters for Me.* New York: Harper & Row, 1981.

Roy, Ron. *What Has Ten Legs and Eats Corn Flakes?* Merlin, OR: Clarion, 1982.

Smyth, Gwenda. *A Pet for Mrs. Arbuckle.* Southbridge, MA: Crown, 1984.

Steinberg, Phil. *You and Your Pet: Terrarium Pets.* Minneapolis: Lerner, 1979.

Viorst, Judith. *If I Were in Charge of the World and Other Worries.* New York: Atheneum, 1981.

Zweifel, Frances W. *Bony.* New York: Harper & Row, 1977.

INVENTIONS

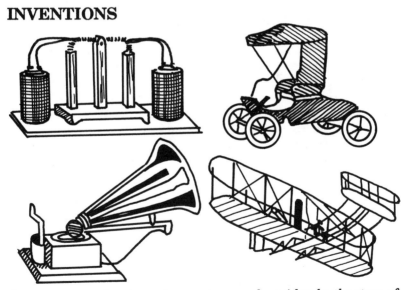

In many ways, the story of a country may be said to be the story of invention. The inventions theme touches the history of a nation's rise to greatness and encourages the spirit of ingenuity. Provide children with the opportunity of viewing books on inventions before beginning the following activities.

232 **Invention Fair** Encourage students to bring junk items to school for an inventions center. Ask students to create their own inventions using parts of the junk items. Have students prepare diagrams explaining how their inventions work. Help students make a display of the inventions. Invite visitors to the exhibit.

233 **Everyday Inventions** Write the names of common inventions on slips of paper. A few common inventions include zippers, eggbeaters, and flashlights. Have students select a slip of paper. Then have students write explanations of the inventions selected without using the name of the object in the description. Next, have students exchange descriptions. Ask children to read the descriptions and name the inventions.

234 **A Timeline of Common Inventions** Help children make a list of common inventions. Ask students to research the inventions. Then help the class make a timeline of the inventions. With the class, make a list of famous people. Ask students whether certain famous people might have used some of the common inventions. For example, could George Washington have used a telephone or could Abraham Lincoln have had a doorbell?

235 **Inventions After 1900** Have students research and make a list of five inventions that did not exist before 1900. Then ask students to write how one of the inventions has affected their lives. When the writings are complete, ask students to share their ideas.

Recommended Books

Aaseng, Nathan. *The Inventors: Nobel Prizes in Chemistry, Physics, and Medicine.* Minneapolis: Lerner, 1988.

Aaseng, Nathan. *The Unsung Heroes: Unheralded People Who Invented Famous Products.* Minneapolis: Lerner, 1989.

Campbell, Hannah. *Why Did They Name It?* New York: Fleet, 1964.

Caney, Steven. *Steven Caney's Invention Book.* New York: Workman, 1985.

Crump, Donald J., ed. *How Things Work.* Washington, D.C.: National Geographic, 1983.

Crump, Donald J., ed. *Small Inventions That Make a Big Difference.* Washington, D.C.: National Geographic, 1984.

Madsen, Sheila and Gould, Betty. *The Teacher's Book of Lists.* Glenview, IL: Scott Foresman, 1979.

Math, Irwin. *Wires and Watts: Using and Understanding Electricity.* New York: Scribners, 1988.

Schulz, Charles M. *Charlie Brown's Fifth Super Book of Questions and Answers: About All Kinds of Things and How They Work!* New York: Random House, 1981.

HOUSES AROUND THE WORLD

Exploring houses around the world will give children an opportunity to see how other people live. In turn, the study will help children better understand their own families and environment. Many of the activities may be adapted to understand how and why animals, insects, and birds build certain types of houses, too.

236 **House References** Collect and display books, magazines, and reference materials related to houses. View and discuss the materials as a class. Ask students to share any reference materials they may have at home.

237 **Types of Houses** Help the class list the many kinds of houses found in their community. A few examples are single dwellings, apartments, condominiums, and mobile homes. Discuss possible reasons for building each type of house and why particular types of material are used in construction. Have students draw pictures of their own houses, labeling its type, and the materials used in construction.

238

World Houses Ask students to research the types of houses built in countries other than their own. Make a class chart that includes the type of house, country, and construction materials. View the chart when complete and discuss possible reasons for types of construction and materials used. Have students select one of the houses to research and report on. Ask students to include such details as climate and terrain, construction materials used, and other details that relate to the types of houses. Ask volunteers to draw small sketches of their researched homes to place on the chart.

239

House Construction Collect pictures of houses across the country for a bulletin-board display. If possible, invite a local contractor to come speak to the class. Ask the speaker to explain why various types of materials are used in house construction. Arrange the class into groups of two or three students. Ask the groups to choose one type of house to research and construct. Houses may be constructed from cardboard, clay, styrofoam, wood, or other appropriate materials. Once research is completed, help students draw plans for construction. Plans should include the types of materials to be used as well as the tasks assigned to each member of the group. Ask that the models be accompanied by a description of the structure, where it would be found, and why that type of house is built.

Recommended Books

Carter, Katharine. *Houses.* Chicago: Childrens Press, 1982.

Huntington, Lee P. *Americans at Home: Four Hundred Years of American Houses.* New York: Coward, 1980.

Jenness, Aylette and Rivers, Alice. *In Two Worlds: A Yupik Eskimo Family.* Boston: Houghton Mifflin, 1989.

Levinson, Riki. *Our Home Is the Sea.* New York: E. P. Dutton, 1988.

Schulz, Charles M. *Charlie Brown's Fourth Super Book of Questions and Answers: About All Kinds of People and How They Live!* New York: Random House, 1979.

Siberell, Anne. *Houses: Shelters from Prehistoric Times to Today.* New York: Holt, 1979.

Yue, Charlotte and Yue, David. *The Igloo.* Boston: Houghton Mifflin, 1988.

NATIVE AMERICANS

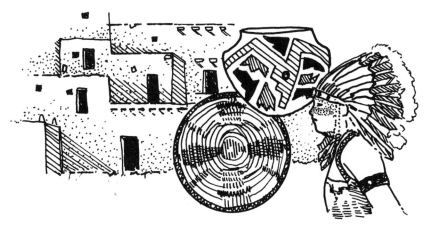

Native Americans are a vital part of the history and growth of this country. Helping children understand and appreciate the Native American culture helps develop an acceptance of the cultural diversity of all nationalities.

240

Native American Houses Have students research historical Native American houses. Hold a class discussion of the dwellings, including where and how they were built and what materials were used. Also, discuss relationships between climate, terrain, available materials, and the types of houses the tribes built.

241

Native American Building Illustrations Have the class draw and color pictures of the various buildings constructed by Native Americans. Encourage students to include an explanation of the building's purpose, construction, and materials used. Display the illustrations on a bulletin board.

242

Native American Foods With the class, explore the kinds of Native American foods eaten in the past, as well as those foods eaten now. Have students draw and label illustrations of the food. Help the class prepare similar food items.

243

Clothing of Native Americans Invite students to study the historical clothing of one tribe, including the materials used, methods of obtaining materials, and how the garments were made. Ask volunteers to illustrate the types of clothing worn by one particular tribe. Arrange the illustrations in a display.

244 **Native American Village** Have students research a historical Native American village. Arrange the class into groups to create dioramas of a Native American village. Use cardboard boxes, sand, clay, small shrubs, and figures to lend realism to the scenes.

245 **Arts and Crafts** Take the class to a museum to study Native American arts and crafts. Or have students research Native American arts and crafts using various resources. Ask some students to draw and color blankets decorated with Native American designs. Ask others to weave baskets or mats from strips of colored paper, raffia, or reeds. Help students create a display of the items.

246 **Map of Native American Tribes** On a large outline map of North America, help the class locate some of the Native American tribes. Ask a volunteer to make a legend for the map.

247 **Native American Legends** Share some Native American legends and tales with the class.

248 **Native Americans and the Colonists** Discuss changes that took place in the Native American community after the arrival of the colonists. Ask students to research some of the following questions: How was Native American life affected by the colonists? Which changes might have been good for the tribe? Which changes might have been bad? Why?

249 **Poems About Native Americans** Ask students to research the Native American way of life during colonial times. Discuss the Native American customs, beliefs, and lifestyles of that time. Have students write descriptive poems about how the Native Americans lived in colonial times using the information they have gathered.

250 **Life As a Native American** Discuss what happened to the Native Americans that once lived in your region. If possible, invite a Native American in the community to speak to the class about Native American life today.

Native American Fair Have the class plan a fair demonstrating the Native American culture in the past and the present. Include crafts, dances, and customs of the past, significant events, such as The Battle of Wounded Knee, and information on the present, including life on a reservation and the American Indian Movement (AIM).

251

Recommended Books

Aliki. *Corn Is Maize: The Gift of the Indians.* New York: Crowell, 1976.

Ashabranner, Brent. *Morning Star, Black Sun.* New York: Putnam, 1982.

Ashabranner, Brent. *To Live in Two Worlds: American Indian Youth Today.* New York: Putnam, 1984.

Brown, Vinson. *Return of the Indian Spirit.* Berkeley, CA: Celestial Arts, 1982.

D'Amato, Janet and D'Amato, Alex. *Indian Crafts.* San Diego. Lion, 1968.

Fritz, Jean. *The Double Life of Pocahontas.* New York: Putnam, 1983.

George, Jean C. *The Talking Earth.* New York: Harper & Row, 1983.

George, Jean C. *The Wild, Wild Cookbook: A Guide for Young Wild Food Foragers.* New York: Crowell, 1982.

Goble, Paul. *Gift of the Sacred Dog.* New York: Macmillan, 1984.

Kessel, Joyce K. *Squanto and the First Thanksgiving.* Minneapolis: Carolrhoda, 1983.

Kroeber, Theodora. *Ishi, Last of His Tribe.* New York: Bantam, 1973.

Levitin, Sonia. *Roanoke.* New York: Atheneum, 1973.

Mayne, William. *Drift.* New York: Dell, 1990.

McDermott, Gerald. *Arrow to the Sun: A Pueblo Indian Tale.* New York: Penguin, 1977.

McGraw, Eloise J. *Moccasin Trail.* New York: Penguin, 1986.

Meyer, Carolyn. *Eskimos: Growing Up in a Changing Culture.* New York: Atheneum, 1977.

Miles, Miska. *Annie and the Old One.* Boston: Little, Brown, 1972.

Nabokov, Peter, ed. *Native American Testimony: An Anthology of Indian and White Relations.* New York: Harper & Row, 1979.

O'Dell, Scott. *Sing Down the Moon*. Boston: Houghton Mifflin, 1970.

Poatgieter, Hermina. *Indian Legacy: Native American Influences on World Life and Culture*. Englewood Cliffs, NJ: Messner, 1981.

Ridington, Jillian and Ridington, Robin. *People of the Longhouse: How the Iroquian Tribes Lived*. Scranton, PA: Salem House, 1982.

San Souci, Robert. *The Legend of Scarface*. New York: Doubleday, 1987.

Sobol, Rose. *Woman Chief*. New York: Dell, 1979.

Speare, Elizabeth G. *Calico Captive*. Boston: Houghton Mifflin, 1957.

Speare, Elizabeth G. *The Sign of the Beaver*. Boston: Houghton Mifflin, 1983.

Tunis, Edwin. *Indians*. New York: Crowell, 1979.

Wheeler, M.J. *First Came the Indians*. New York: McElderry, 1983.

Wolfson, Evelyn. *American Indian Utensils: How to Make Baskets, Pottery and Woodenware with Natural Materials*. New York: McKay, 1979.

Wolfson, Evelyn. *From Abenaki to Zuni: A Dictionary of Native American Tribes*. New York: Walker, 1988.

Yue, Charlotte and Yue, David. *The Pueblo*. Boston: Houghton Mifflin, 1986.

Yue, Charlotte and Yue, David. *The Tipi: A Center of Native American Life*. New York: Knopf, 1984.

EARLY COLONISTS

A study of colonial life helps children understand the basic needs of people. Early colonists were under the governmental control of Great Britain. As a result, the colonists were required to follow the laws of the colony that were set by governors who were controlled by Great Britain. The following activities will help the children see that all people struggle to achieve their wants and needs in life.

252 **Reasons for the Colonists** Ask students to research the following questions: When did the colonists come to the New World? Where did they come from? Why did the colonists come? Why were the members of a new colony important to its success? As a class, discuss the questions and answers. Help students draw conclusions from their research.

253 **Problems of the Colonists** Discuss with the class the landing of the colonists and the immediate problems they faced. A few problems include climate, need for shelter, and lack of food. Also discuss problems that developed during the early days of the colonies. Ask students to research how the colonists organized their colonies, including the laws and government.

254 **Types of Colonists' Houses** As a class, study the types of houses the colonists built. Discuss how building styles were related to the terrain and availability of materials. Ask the students to compare the colonists' dwellings to the Native American dwellings built in the area.

255 **Models of Colonists' Houses** Discuss the materials the colonists used to build their houses. Help the class make a list of supplies needed to make models of the colonists' houses. Allow time for students to build model houses. Display the completed houses.

256 **Foods of the Colonists** Have children research the kinds of foods the colonists ate. Ask whether colonists ate the same type of foods that the Native Americans ate or whether their foods were different. Suggest that students use old cookbooks to find recipes that might have been handed down from ancestors. Ask if any similar foods are eaten today. Help students plan and cook a meal a colonist family might have eaten.

257 **Clothing of the Colonists** Suggest that students research and draw pictures showing how the colonists dressed. Ask the students to consider the following questions: What methods did the colonists use to make new clothing in the New World? Why were the colonists' children so careful with their clothing? As a class, write a short report combining the information the students gathered in their research.

258 **Colonists and the Native Americans** Read aloud to the class about the colonists' relationship with the Native Americans. Discuss the ways the two groups became acquainted, the type of relationship that developed, and the advantages of the relationship. Also ask what were some disadvantages with the groups living close to one another.

259 **Education in the Colonies** Have the class research education in the early colonies. Help students make hornbooks for their lessons. Discuss what colonial methods of teaching and classroom management should be used. Help the students compare the colonial school with today's schools.

260 **Government of the Colonies** Discuss with the class the problems of creating a government. Ask students to research the following questions: How did the colonists create their government? What was the *Mayflower Compact*? What kind of government did the colonists organize? What part did women play in establishing the new government? How is government different today? After researching the questions, hold a class discussion.

261 **A Plymouth Colony Mural** Help children research the town that developed in the Plymouth colony. Have children make rough sketches of the church, school, stores, and blockhouse. Help students plan a mural of the town using their research and sketches. Provide the class with butcher paper, markers, crayons, glue, and construction paper. Have students create a mural of the town. Display the mural in a hallway.

262 **View Colonial Life** If possible, take the class to a museum that has a display of colonial life. Ask students to examine the display carefully, noting dress, tools, and equipment. Some museums offer demonstrations of crafts and daily activities, such as weaving, spinning, or churning.

263

Drama of Colonial Life Help the class plan a dramatization of life in an early colony as a culminating activity. Include scenes representing all aspects of daily life. A few scenes might be home, school, work, and recreation. Invite parents or another class as guests.

Recommended Books

Anderson, Joan. *A Williamsburg Household.* Merlin, OR: Clarion, 1988.

Anderson, Joan. *Pioneer Children of Appalachia.* Merlin, OR: Clarion, 1986.

Clapp, Patricia C. *Constance.* New York: Penguin, 1986.

Earle, Alice M. *Home Life in Colonial Days.* Williams, MA: Corner House, 1975.

Freedman, Russell. *Children of the Wild West.* Merlin, OR: Clarion, 1983.

Henry, Joanne L. and Zarins, Joyce A. *Log Cabin in the Woods: A True Story About a Pioneer Boy.* New York: Four Winds, 1988.

Kinney, Jean and Kinney, Cle. *21 Kinds of American Folk Art and How to Make Each One.* New York: Atheneum, 1972.

Lobel, Arnold. *On the Day Peter Stuyvesant Sailed into Town.* New York: Harper & Row, 1971.

Payne, Elizabeth. *Meet the Pilgrim Fathers.* New York: Random House, 1966.

Perl, Lila. *Slumps, Grunts, and Snickerdoodles: What Colonial America Ate and Why.* Merlin, OR: Clarion, 1979.

Richards, Norman. *The Story of the Mayflower Compact.* Chicago: Childrens Press, 1967.

Sewall, Marcia. *The Pilgrims of Plimoth.* New York: Macmillan, 1986.

Seymour, John. *The Forgotten Crafts.* New York: Knopf, 1984.

Siegel, Beatrice. *A New Look at the Pilgrims: Why They Came to America.* New York: Walker, 1977.

Speare, Elizabeth G. *The Witch of Blackbird Pond.* New York: Dell, 1987.

Tunis, John. *Colonial Living.* New York: Crowell, 1976.

Tunis, John. *Frontier Living.* New York: Crowell, 1976.

Tunis, John. *The Tavern at the Ferry.* New York: Crowell, 1973.

Walket, Jr., John J. and Ford, Thomas K. *A Window on Williamsburg.* Williamsburg, VA: Colonial Williamsburg Foundation, 1966.

Wisler, Clifton G. *This New Land.* New York: Walker, 1987.

FOLKTALES

It has been said that folktales reflect the lives, customs, beliefs, and emotions of a people. Folktales teach kindness, industry, morality, and courage and create dramatic examples of good and bad behavior, as well as social and moral standards. A study of the folklore of any country or culture can be an enlightening and enjoyable experience at any grade level.

264 **Sharing Folktales** Share folktales of a culture being studied. Help students identify social practices and cultural beliefs in the tales. Compare these practices and beliefs with those of other cultures already studied. Help the class draw conclusions about the society under study and document the conclusions with references from the tales.

265 **Comparing Folktales** Have students read folktales from many lands. Discuss the similarities and the differences in the stories. Then discuss possible reasons for the similarities and differences.

266 **Origin of Folktales** Help students research the origins of folktales, how the stories were passed on, and who the storytellers originally were. Hold a class discussion using the students' research. Help students draw conclusions of how the written versions came to be.

267 **Folktale Dramatization** Discuss dramatizing folktales. Arrange the students into small groups. Have the groups choose folktales to dramatize. Suggest that two groups dramatize the same folktale from different countries. Invite another class to view the folktale dramatizations.

268 **Storytellers** Invite a professional storyteller to share some folktales with the class. Students may wish to share some of the stories they have learned on their own with the storyteller. Have students write original folktales.

269 **Folktale Mobiles** Arrange the class into groups of four or five. Have the groups choose folktales to illustrate. Ask the groups to create illustrations of characters and

representative objects from the folktales for their
mobiles. Display the mobiles in the classroom.

Folktale Puppets Have the class make and use
puppets to retell folktales. A variety of puppets might
include finger puppets, paper-bag puppets, and stick
puppets.

270

Recommended Books

Aesop. *Aesop's Fables*. Southbridge, MA: Crown, 1988.

Asbjornsen, Peter and Moe, Jorgen E. *Norwegian Folk Tales*. New
York: Pantheon, 1982.

Carpenter, Frances. *Tales of a Korean Grandmother*. Rutland,
VT: Tuttle, 1972.

Chase, Richard. *Jack Tales*. Boston: Houghton Mifflin, 1943.

Coburn, Jewell R. *Beyond the East Wind: Legends and Folktales
of Vietnam*. Thousand Oaks, CA: Burn Hart, 1976.

Coburn, Jewell R. *Encircled Kingdom: Legends and Folktales of
Laos*. Thousand Oaks, CA: Burn Hart, 1979.

Courlander, Harold. *The Crest and the Hide and Other African
Stories*. New York: Coward, 1982.

Courlander, Harold. *The King's Drum and Other African Stories*.
San Diego: Harcourt Brace Jovanovich, 1962.

D'Aulaire, Ingri and D'Aulaire, Edgar P. *D'Aulaire's Book of
Greek Myths*. New York: Doubleday, 1980.

D'Aulaire, Ingri and D'Aulaire, Edgar P. *D'Aulaire's Norse Gods
and Giants*. New York: Doubleday, 1986.

Deroin, Nancy. *Jataka Tales*. Boston: Houghton Mifflin, 1975.

Haley, Gail E. A *Story, a Story*. New York: Atheneum, 1970.

Jaquith, Priscilla. *Bo Rabbit Smart for True: Folktales from the
Gullah*. New York: Philomel, 1981.

Kamerman, Sylvia, ed. *Plays from Favorite Folk Tales*. Boston:
Plays, Inc., 1971.

McCormick, Dell J. *Paul Bunyan Swings His Axe*. Caldwell, ID:
Caxton, 1936.

McDermott, Gerald. *Anansi the Spider: A Tale from the Ashanti*.
New York: Holt, 1972.

Nolan, Paul T. *Folk Tale Plays Round the World*. Boston: Plays,
1982.

Reeves, James. *English Fables and Fairy Stories*. New York:
Oxford, 1989.

Stoutenberg, Adrien. *American Tall Tales*. New York: Penguin,
1966.

Uchida, Yoshiko. *The Magic Listening Cap*. Fort Lauderdale:

Creative Arts, 1987.

Young, Ed. *Lon Po Po: A Red Riding Hood Story from China.* New York: Philomel, 1989.

Zemach, Margot. *It Could Always Be Worse.* Tacoma, WA: Sunburst, 1990.

THE SEA

The sea theme is particularly adaptable for use at different grade levels, depending upon the depth of subject matter and complexity of activities introduced. Arrange a display of books and pictures to motivate the students' interest in the sea.

271

Sea Discussion Display a world map in the classroom. As a large group, discuss and list the various seas and oceans. Help students list the advantages of a country having a sea border. Determine which countries have long coastlines. Ask the students to consider the advantages and disadvantages of having a coastline.

272

Sea Life As a class, list various kinds of sea life. Kinds of sea life might include fish, mammals, crustaceans, seaweed, and birds. Arrange the class into small groups. Have the groups choose one type of sea life to research. Ask the groups to write summaries of their findings on the habitat, life cycles, and the place in the food chain of their subjects. Have the groups read their reports aloud to the class.

273

Tide Pools If possible, visit or research a local tide pool. Have students take notes about the sea life found in a tide pool. Hold a class discussion using the students notes. Display a collection of sea life found in a tide pool in the classroom. The display might include actual sea life or student illustrations.

274

Visit an Aquarium Before the visit, help students develop a list of questions about aquarium life. Use the questions for class discussion on returning to the classroom. As a class, make a bulletin-board aquarium. Have the students make drawings of sea life seen at the aquarium to put on the bulletin board.

275 **Study a Sea Creature** Have students choose different sea creatures to study. After gathering information about the sea creatures, have students prepare talks for the class. Encourage the students to make illustrations to accompany their talks.

276 **Sea Life Mural** Help the students plan a mural of sea life. Encourage students to create as many creatures as possible, using a variety of shapes and colors to show fish, shellfish, coral, and seaweed. Display the mural in a hallway.

277 **Sea Creature Mobiles** Have students create mobiles with sea creatures cut from colored paper. Encourage students to include fish, dolphins, seals, pelicans, sea gulls, and seaweed. Hang the mobiles in the classroom.

278 **A Bulletin-Board Display** Help the class make a display of objects or foods we use from the oceans and seas. The students might find objects in pictures, brochures, labels, advertisements, and newspaper items.

279 **Sea Writings** As a class, listen to recordings and sing songs about the sea. Then have children write descriptive paragraphs or poems.

280 **Sea Recreation** Have students investigate recreational activities related to the sea. A few activities include snorkeling, sailing, and fishing. Encourage the class to collect brochures describing the various types of equipment, clothing, and regions in which the sports are found. Have students write brief descriptions of their findings. Create a display of the descriptions and brochures.

281 **Commercial Fishing** Invite students to browse through almanacs for information about the economic aspects of commercial fishing. List the following questions on a chart for the class to research: Which countries depend heavily upon the fishing industry to support their economies? What international problems exist because of disagreements about fishing rights? What solutions are being suggested? What is the three-mile limit? How does the three-mile limit affect peaceful relationships among fishing nations? Hold a class discussion after the students have completed their research. Complete the chart with the answers found. As a class, write an article about commercial fishing.

282 **Civilization's Abuse of the Sea** Invite a marine biologist or environmentalist to speak to the class on "Civilization's Abuse of the Sea." Ask students to take notes while the speaker talks. After the presentation, have students write a one-paragraph summary of the presentation. Encourage discussion.

Recommended Books

Clemons, Elizabeth. *Waves, Tides, and Currents.* New York: Knopf, 1967.

Hargreaves, Pat. *The Antarctic.* Englewood Cliffs, NJ: Silver Burdett, 1980.

Lampton, Christopher. *Endangered Species.* New York: Watts, 1988.

Lewis, C. S. *The Voyage of the "Dawn Treader."* New York: Macmillan, 1988.

O'Dell, Scott. *Island of the Blue Dolphins.* Boston: Houghton Mifflin, 1960.

Oxford Scientific Film Editors. *Jellyfish and Other Sea Creatures.* New York: Putnam, 1982.

Patent, Dorothy H. *All About Whales.* New York: Holiday, 1987.

Simon, Hilda. *Snails of Land and Sea.* New York: Vanguard, 1976.

Simon, Seymour. *How to Be an Ocean Scientist in Your Own Home.* Philadelphia: Lippincott, 1988.

Simon, Seymour. *Whales.* New York: Crowell, 1989.

MAPS

Map reading may be taught at any grade level by introducing appropriate skills and materials. This theme has been developed, offering a wide variety of activities from which to choose. Create a display of various maps and globes to encourage students' interest in maps. A few types of maps include physical, political, population, and weather.

283 **Map Discussion** Discuss maps used in everyday life. Ask students what maps they or their families have used recently and how they were used. Make a list on chart paper of the maps and their uses. Encourage students to add to the chart as the study progresses. If possible, visit a local planning commission to see how maps are used by this organization.

284 **Maps and Their Uses** Ask students to bring two different maps to class. Have children study their maps and share two things they have learned from each map. Add the uses to the list already started in the previous activity.

285 **Physical and Political Maps** Help children compare physical maps with political maps. Show the class a variety of maps. Ask the children to state whether the maps are physical or political.

286 **World Maps** On a large world map, help the class locate land and water masses. Ask students the names of the continents and oceans. Discuss directions on the maps. Locate the North and South Poles. Help children locate the continent on which the class lives, the country, and the neighboring countries. Locate the state or province in which the community exists and find the approximate location of the community. Discuss the directional location of the school community in relation to the state, province, or country.

287 **Lines on a Map** With the class, locate and discuss the lines on a world map. The lines include latitude, longitude, Equator, Tropic of Cancer, Tropic of Capricorn, Arctic Circle, and Antarctic Circle. Ask students to research the uses of the lines in relation to navigation. Provide students with blank world maps. Ask students to locate the lines on their maps.

288 **Map Projections** Discuss the names of the various map projections. Some map projections include Mercator, Lambert conformal conic, Mollweide equal area, and polyconic. Arrange the class in small groups. Ask the groups to research one of the map projections. When research is complete, ask the groups to explain the various map projections to the class.

289 **Map Legends** Have students compare and use legends on different types of maps. Discuss symbols used on road maps to represent cities of different sizes, rivers, coastlines, canals, roads, highways, railroads, and parks. Arrange the class in groups of two or three. Have the groups practice measuring distances between selected locations. Encourage the groups to compare the distances.

290

A Map to School Provide the class with copies of city or neighborhood maps. Ask students to locate their homes and the school. Ask the class to write directions from their homes to school on a separate piece of paper. This may be done by naming the streets and giving north, south, east, and west directions. When students have completed their directions, ask them to exchange directions with other students. Ask the students to follow the directions using their copies of the map. Directions may need to be revised to be accurate.

291

Using Atlases Show the class several atlases. Discuss the uses of atlases. For example, atlases help in the location and identification of geographical features and provide information on boundaries, climate, population, resources, languages, and vegetation. Allow time for students to practice using the atlases. Ask questions that will encourage the children to search for the answers using several of the maps in the atlases.

292

School Maps Provide the class with paper to draw freehand maps of the school. Discuss the students' maps. Repeat the assignment, using a simple scale, such as one-fourth inch equals one foot. Compare the two maps and discuss the importance of using a scale.

Recommended Books

Arnold, Carolyn. *Maps and Globes: Fun, Facts, and Activities.* New York: Watts, 1984.

Bell, Neill. *The Book of Where: Or How to Be Naturally Geographic.* Boston: Little, Brown, 1982.

Broekel, Ray. *Maps and Globes.* Chicago: Childrens Press, 1983.

Knowlton, Jack. *Maps and Globes.* New York: Harper & Row, 1986.

Madden, James F. *The Wonderful World of Maps.* Maplewood, NJ: Hammond, 1986.

Mango, Karin N. *Mapmaking.* Englewood Cliffs, NJ: Messner, 1984.

QUESTIONS TO STIMULATE BOOK DISCUSSIONS

Because most of the activities in this book grow out of discussion, here are a few suggestions for questions to stimulate thinking and motivate interaction.

Character

- How did the characters face difficulty?
- What were their relationships with others?
- What were their strongest characteristics?
- Which character did you think was strongest? Why? Which one did you think was weakest? Why?
- Compare the characters in different books. How are the characters alike? How are they different?
- How do you think the characters from different books would have acted if they had met? Do you think they would have gotten along well? Explain your answers.
- How would the characters in a given book have responded to the situation in another book? Would they have responded in the same way as the actual book's characters did? Explain why or why not.

Plot

- How did the author sustain the reader's interest?
- How did the author build the story to a climax?
- How did the author create an atmosphere for the story?

Style

- How did the author build the characters?
- How did the author use dialogue to describe a character? Read an example.
- Why was one book more interesting, more exciting, sadder, harder, or easier to read than another? Give examples.
- After having read several books by the same author, do you notice any typical characteristics or patterns in the stories? Describe them.

SUGGESTIONS FOR SUCCESSFUL GROUP WORK

Group work can be enjoyable for both the students and the teacher if a few simple guidelines are followed. These guidelines are based on wide experience in conducting group work at all grade levels and with many types of students.

1. Plan! Think through what you expect to accomplish with this group work and how you expect to accomplish it. Stop to reflect for a few moments on your objectives for group work. They might include learning to develop initiative, assume responsibility, share ideas, respect the talents of others, develop leadership abilities, work independently, or work well within a group. In the process of attaining these objectives, students will gain knowledge in a broad spectrum of subject areas and skills.

2. Divide the class into groups of a workable size—usually not more than five; three works best. Because the students should select the project on which they will work, the size of the groups may vary. Pay attention to the composition of the groups. As the teacher, you know that to assure maximum learning, certain students should not work together. In this case, a simple "Jack, today Bill's group needs you to work with them" is usually effective if said casually and with a certain amount of firmness.

3. Appoint a leader for each group. Again, do it casually. This is not being dictatorial—it is part of your direction of and involvement in the activity. Select someone you know who is reliable and will see that the group works to complete its project. Be sure to give as many students as possible a chance to be the group leader. The leader can also have the responsibility of stopping work at the agreed-upon time for clean-up and seeing that all is left in order. The leader is your liaison with each group when you need to check on plans or progress, or when the group needs to communicate with you. Playing the role of group leader is good leadership training, which is an important objective of group work.

4. Once the members of each group have decided on their project, have them prepare a sketch or outline of what they plan to do. This is the time for you to evaluate the scope of their plans. Are

their plans realistic? Is the project too easy or too complex? Are the necessary materials available? Can it be completed in the allotted time? Help the group adjust its plans, if necessary. This will assure an orderly procedure and avoid confusion and delay when the work period begins.

5. At the beginning of the work period, check with the leader of each group to be sure that they know what they are going to do and that the needed materials are available. It's a good idea to remind the leaders to check on each member of their group individually. These are the kinds of details that can make or break an activity period!

6. Once the work period has begun, the noise level will rise. When it gets too loud, call for a minute of silence. Then begin work again with a reminder that it is necessary to use soft voices when so many people are working.

7. Decide on a quitting time before the work begins to allow time for clean-up, evaluation of work accomplished, and planning the project's next steps.

8. Make sure every project is completed unless an unavoidable situation prevents it. An unfinished project usually indicates it was begun with no real objective in mind.

9. Have material ready for an alternative activity in the event that one group cannot work on its activity or that it finishes ahead of the others. An art activity is usually a good choice—for example, creating a picture related to the theme with paints, crayons, or cut paper or cutting out and mounting as a collage pictures or parts of pictures related to the theme or to a story. Whatever the alternative activity, it should be related to the theme and it should be one that was previously demonstrated to keep disruption of the work session minimal.

BIBLIOGRAPHY

Austin, Mary C. and Jenkins, Esther. *Promoting World Understanding Through Literature, K-8.* Englewood, CO: Libraries Unlimited, 1983.

Bauer, Caroline F. *Celebrations: Read-Aloud Holiday and Theme Book Programs.* New York: Wilson, 1985.

Blough, Glenn O. and Schwartz, Julius. *Elementary School Science and How to Teach It.* New York: Holt, 1984.

Huck, Charlotte S. *Children's Literature in the Elementary School.* New York: Holt, 1987.

King, Edith W. *Teaching Ethnic and Gender Awareness: Methods and Materials for the Elementary School.* Dubuque, IA: Kendall-Hunt, 1989.

Kobrin, Beverly. *Eyeopeners! How to Choose and Use Children's Books About Real People, Places, and Things.* New York: Penguin, 1988.

Labuda, Michael, ed. *Creative Reading for Gifted Learners.* Newark: International Reading Association, 1985.

Lima, Carolyn W. *A to Zoo: Subject Access to Children's Picture Books.* New York: Bowker, 1989.

Literature in the Elementary Language Arts Committee and Linda Lamme. *Learning to Love Literature: Pre-School through Grade 3.* Urbana, IL: National Council of Teachers of English, 1981.

Norton, Donna E. *Through the Eyes of a Child: An Introduction to Children's Literature.* Columbus: Merrill, 1983.

Olsen, Mary L. *Creative Connections: Literature and the Reading Program, Grades 1-3.* Englewood, CO: Libraries Unlimited, 1987.

Polette, Nancy. *3 R's for the Gifted: Reading, Writing, and Research.* Englewood, CO: Libraries Unlimited, 1982.

Reading for Young People Series. Chicago: American Library Association, 1980.

Schon, Isabel. *A Bicultural Heritage: Themes for the Exploration of Mexican and Mexican-American Culture in Books for Children and Adolescents.* Metuchen, NJ: Scarecrow, 1978.

Tooze, Ruth and Krone, Beatrice P. *Literature and Music As Resources for the Social Studies.* Westport, CT: Greenwood, 1974.

Winkel, Lois, ed. *The Elementary School Library Collection.* Williamsport, PA: Brodart, 1988.

PERIODICALS FOR
TEACHERS AND CHILDREN

For Teachers:

Early American Life. Historical Times, Inc., 2245 Kohn Rd., Box
8200, Harrisburg, PA 17105. A bi-monthly magazine devoted to
arts, crafts, collecting, and furnishings.

Science and Children. National Science Teachers Association,
1742 Connecticut Ave. N.W., Washington, D.C. 20009. Includes
suggestions for units and projects, information on trends in
science, teaching, reviews of books, and instructional materials.
Eight issues per year for the elementary classroom teacher.

Science News. 1719 N. Street N.W., Washington, D.C. 20036.
Weekly issues report on current developments in science.

Social Education. Journal of the National Council for Social
Studies, 3501 Newark St. N.W., Washington, D.C. 20016.
Twelve volumes per year keep elementary teachers up-to-date
on issues and trends in social studies instruction and provide
cross-grade topics and projects, as well as a listing of new
books and materials.

For Children:

Cobblestone: The History Magazine for Young People. Cobblestone
Publishing, Inc., 20 Grove St., Peterborough, NH 03458.
Monthly magazine on American history for ages 8-14.

Faces: The Magazine About People. Cobblestone Publishing,
Inc., 20 Grove St., Peterborough, NH 03458. Anthropological
magazine for ages 8-14. Each of the ten issues per year is
devoted to one culture, with pictures, recipes, information on all
aspects of the society.

National Geographic World. National Geographic Society, 17th &
M Streets N.W., Washington, D.C. 20036. A monthly magazine
that features factual stories on outdoors, adventure, natural
history, sports, science, and history for children ages 8-13.

Penny Power. Consumers Union of the U. S., Inc., 256 Washington
Street, Mount Vernon, NY 10553. A child's guide to spending
and saving. Six issues per year.

About the Authors

Evangeline Drury Geiger graduated from Lowell University in Massachusetts with a bachelor's degree in education. After teaching for several years, she moved to California where she earned a master's degree at San Francisco State University and a doctorate from the University of California, Berkeley. She began her teaching career in Vermont in a one-room school with 27 children in six different grades. Since then, she has taught every grade from 1 through 8, plus classes in dramatics, art, and music in Massachusetts and California. She has also been an elementary and intermediate school administrator, a curriculum consultant for grades K-12, and a professor of education at Sonoma State University, where she has been honored with the title Emeritus. She has served as a member of the board of directors of the California Reading Association and as editor of the *California Reader*.

Beverley Fonnesbeck graduated from Occidental College, Los Angeles, with a bachelor's degree in English Literature and secondary teaching. After teaching secondary and elementary classes on the California desert, she moved to the San Francisco Bay Area. Dr. Fonnesbeck then moved to Anchorage, Alaska, where she has been an elementary school librarian since 1968. During her career, she has received a master's degree from San Francisco State University and a doctorate from the University of Southern California, as well as completing library work at the University of San Francisco. Dr. Fonnesbeck has been a teacher in the demonstration school at San Jose State University and has served in teacher training programs for San Francisco State University and the Dominican College of San Rafael. She has taught children's literature at Alaska Pacific University, is a charter member of the Anchorage School District Talent Bank, has been active in the Anchorage Writing Project, and recently completed a two-year membership on the Alaska State Literature Panel.

Lincoln Township Library
2099 W. John Beers Rd.
Stevensville, MI 49127
429-9575